Captured by Calvary

31 Biblical Devotions to Meditate on the Cross - God's Glory

Dedication

To the memory of a faithful disciple

A wise Elder

A great friend

Tom Fraser from Black Hill, NSW.

About Ray Hawkins

A Rockdale boy (NSW) who was an early Christmas present to his parents being born 18th.12.1938. He grew up in a working class home, worked as a lathe operator for a car engine repair firm then a labourer with his father's light steel fabrication business and was sent to Sunday school at the local Church of Christ where he made his confession of faith and was baptized. At 21 years he was accepted as a student at the Churches of Christ Woolwich Bible College (Sydney). In 1963 Ray became the Student President of the College. That year he met his wife to be, Mary, who came to College for a two year missionary course. In 1964 they were married and over the years they became parents of three children.

Their major ministry emphasis has been in establishing 2 new Churches in N.S.W. and preventing one from closure in Qld. They also ministered in England. Ray has been N.S.W. Conference President on two occasions, and N.S.W. President for the Ministers' Association. He has been a Chaplain to the Green Hills Retirement village and Nursing Home (N.S.W.). For 18 years he was involved with the Tenambit/Morpeth Rotary club becoming President and later made a 'Paul Harris Fellow'. Ray also became active with the 'Walk to Emmaus' movement and was Community Spiritual Director for Tasmania.

In his later years he went with Mary three times as part of short term mission trips to Africa. Out of that experience he wrote the 31 day devotional 'The Neurotic Rooster.' (It was a finance raiser for Eagles Wings in Zambia.) Now retired to Beauty Point, Tasmania, with Mary who is a multi-published Inspirational Romance writer he still preaches and is involved in establishing a Christian Fellowship there.

He is a regular contributor to 'The Upper Room' devotional magazine as well as having numerous articles, poems and Studies from Scripture printed throughout his ministry. More information about Ray on www.mary-hawkins.com.

Captured by Calvary
Published by Even Before Publishing;
a division of Wombat Books
P. O. Box 1519, Capalaba Qld 4157
www.evenbeforepublishing.com
www.wombatbooks.com.au

© Ray Hawkins 2012
Design and layout by Even Before Publishing

ISBN: 978-1-922074-00-3

National Library of Australia Cataloguing-in-Publication entry included in Australia

All rights reserved. No part of this publication may be reproduced, stored in, or introduced into a retrieval system, or transmitted, in any form, or by any means (electronic, mechanical, photocopying, recording or otherwise) without the prior written permission of the publisher.

Unless otherwise indicated all Bible quotes are from the New International Version.

Contents

About Ray Hawkins	*1*
Introduction	*8*
Creation and the Cross	*10*

Day 1
The Cross before Time — *12*

Day 2
The Cosmic conflict of Passover — *14*

Day 3
Strange Glory — *16*

Day 4
Lifted Up — *18*

Day 5
Now is the Hour — *20*

Day 6
By His Stripes — *22*

Day 7
The Blood of the Covenant — *24*

Day 8
Father Forgive them — *26*

Day 9
Look and Live — *28*

Day 10
The Curtain is Torn — *30*

Day 11
The Cup and the Cross — *32*

Day 12
: *The Tree* — *34*

Day 13
: *The Triumph of the Cross* — *36*

Day 14
: *Co-Crucified* — *38*

Date 15
: *How God Accepts* — *40*

Day 16
: *The Cross begins our Journey* — *42*

Day 17
: *Something for God the Father* — *44*

Day 18
: *The Cross and 'The Stone'* — *46*

Day 19
: *My God is Weak* — *48*

Day 20
: *My Boast* — *51*

Day 21
: *Validating the Cross* — *54*

Day 22
: *Racism and the Cross* — *57*

Day 23
: *Good News* — *59*

Day 24
: *The Suffering and the Glory.* — *61*

Day 25
- *The Cross and the Coming King* — *63*

Day 26
- *The Foolishness of God* — *65*

Day 27
- *Those Symbolised around the Cross* — *67*

Day 28
- *The Personal Mystery of the Cross* — *69*

Day 29
- *Heaven's Song of Calvary* — *71*

Day 30
- *My Personal Cross* — *73*

Day 31
- *Heaven's Song to the Lamb* — *75*

Introduction

The following 31 day devotionals are meant to deepen your understanding and increase your love for the Lord Jesus. As you reflect upon what the Lord achieved for you at Calvary, the horror of the cross is transformed into Christ's glory. It is also our assurance of salvation. The cross for the Christian is an expression of glory and wonder.

Why?

Because it speaks of God's grace, love and majesty!

The message of the crucified Christ comforts because it deals with the issues between us and the Almighty.

It humbles because it says Jesus alone could solve our sin and condemnation problem.

It compels a man or woman to commit his or her life to Jesus. It calls us to leave the realm of darkness, take up our cross and follow Him.

The cross is a stumbling block to many. Their sense of righteousness is offended. The effectiveness of their religion is undermined. For others the cross becomes the stepping stone into a new relationship of grace, a new destiny with the Lord God, a new sense of their worth.

There are two roads the Church can travel as it reaches out into the community. The road most appreciated by any community would be the way the Good Samaritan travelled. He cared for the oppressed and vulnerable. When the Church serves this way it doesn't upset people or create waves of antagonism.

The other road is nowhere near as popular or appealing. It is the way of the Cross. This is no scenic route. It is gruesome. It is threatening. It is uncompromising. And yet it is this very road which brings people out of spiritual and moral darkness and into the light of God's grace. It is along this way that the Holy Spirit attracts the heart of people with the wonder of a new beginning, the hope of a greater destiny.

Why?

Because it shows the way to be transformed, made acceptable to God! The individual is liberated to worship the God of Grace and Glory.

Both roads are important.

However, the Faith Community must major on what the Apostle Paul considers the power and wisdom of God. This is the road we enter upon when we are captured by the Christ of Calvary.

Raymond N Hawkins.

Creation and the Cross

Day 1

Key verse: *The creation waits in eager expectation for the sons of God to be revealed (then) the creation itself will be liberated from its bondage to decay and brought into the glorious freedom of the children of God. Romans 8:19, 21.*

Six days it took for God to create the world and proclaim it very good. One moment of rebellion shattered it all. The account in Genesis chapters 1-3 is simple, sometimes terse, and to the point. Adam's sin is so profound, it not only enveloped his offspring, it tainted all of creation. The Lord God then cursed the ground which turned some of what was pronounced 'good' into thorns and weeds. The extent of what Adam did spread out into the heavens.

'If God places no trust in his holy ones, if even the heavens are not pure in his eyes, how much less man, who is vile and corrupt and drinks up evil like water' (Job 15:15-16).

Why are the heavens impure?

Many of the constellations, including the signs of the Zodiac, became objects of worship and subjects of idolatry. (Jeremiah 7:18).

Compounding this tragedy we are told in Ephesians 2:2 that Satan set up his control centre 'in the air.' Since that time the universe has been under the sentence of extinction. 'They will perish, but you remain; they will all wear out like a garment. Like clothing you will change them and they will be discarded' (Psalm 102:26).

Further, the actions of humankind has polluted the very ground it has walked upon. (Numbers 35:33). It becomes very apparent that creation has been in bondage and under a curse since that day Adam violated his trust. How easy it is for us to take lightly the doctrine of sin and its wicked and degrading power. This is part of the reason why the Scriptures reveal a new heaven and a new earth are needed and are coming.

Before the Day of the Lord ushers in such a wonderful new creation, the curse on the old creation must be lifted. The prince of the power of the air must be dethroned. The polluted land, saturated by innocent and unrequited blood must be atoned for. How could this happen? Who could bear the curse, purify the heavens and atone for the land?

We know it could only be the Creator who took on our humanity in the event we now call Christmas. In Galatians 3:13 we are told that this Jesus bore the curse of condemnation when he was crucified. Jesus lifted from all humankind and creation the horror begun in Eden. The tree on Calvary provided the 'fruit' for the condemned sinners that would heal them of the curse. It also provided the power to transform the environment into the atmosphere of Eden. Isaiah 11:6-9 describes that time usually called the Millennium: 'The wolf will live with the lamb, the leopard will lie down with the goat, the calf and the lion and the yearling together; and a little child will lead them… The infant will play near the hole of the cobra, and the young child put his hand into the viper's nest… the earth will be full of the knowledge of the Lord…'

In today's key verse Paul seems to give redeemed creation personification as it anticipates the day of liberation. Creation seems to know something more about the future glory than we do. I wonder how?

Reflection: When we say the Lord's Prayer we are praying for our Lord to restore the earth to its initial condition. As you read those verses from Isaiah 11 what are some of the pictures that come to mind?

The Cross before Time

Day 2

Key verse: *You know that it was not with perishable things such as silver or gold that you were redeemed from the empty way of life handed down to you from your fore-fathers, but with the precious blood of Christ, a lamb without blemish or defect. He was chosen before the creation of the world, but was revealed in these last times for your sake. 1 Peter 1:18-20.*

The Lord God's foreknowledge made Him well aware of Adam's future act of treason in Eden. Being expelled from the garden would seem, on the surface, a mild rebuke rather than a judicial decree. The declaration about death also doesn't appear to be very frightening. Only as the record unfolds do we gain an appreciation of the horror and dread sin unleashed. A question remained. How could the holy God still communicate with the expelled couple, and later, their offspring?

Strange though it may be the answer is given in the closing book of the Bible. Revelation 13:8b tells us that the Lamb (a title for Jesus) was slain from the creation of the world. God could only bear with Adam and his offspring because in God's mind the Cross had already taken place. God was able to deal with humanity because He looked at them through the Cross. This is still the only way He can deal with the world.

One day, in His time, the Lord will say, 'It's judgment time!' On that day He won't be looking at people through the cross (read Revelation 20). He will be assessing them from his throne!

An uneasy feeling surrounds dying within the human heart and mind. Passing from this life into the next dimension leads us to an accounting time before God. In the book of Job, one of the friends makes a very pertinent quote, 'How then can a man be righteous before God? How can one born of a woman be pure? If even the moon is not bright and the stars are not pure in his eyes, how much less man…' (Job 25:4-6a).

In Genesis 3 Adam and Eve try to make themselves respectable to God by covering themselves with fig leaves. It was an attempt to camouflage their true condition. There was no repentance and there was no indication of sin's action being atoned.

In Genesis 3:21 is the act of real atonement. The word atonement refers to a covering. 'The Lord God made garments of skin for Adam and his wife and clothed them.' This was provided so as not to be offensive to God and thereby be destroyed. The initiative was God's. It cost the life of a substitute animal. Here is a shadow of God's answer to the quote from Job: the only way to be righteous before God is for someone to pay the price for our covering.

When Revelation 13:8b speaks of 'a Lamb slain' the word for slain refers to an act of slaying for the purpose of sacrifice. Within the sacrificial system of ancient Israel animals were slain as a substitute for the individual or nation. The shadow cast by the sacrificial system of Israel is fulfilled in the crucifixion of Jesus Christ. Before time had begun the Godhead knew the consequences of creation mixed with freewill. God was willing to pay the price!

The Apostle Peter wrote about that in the key verse: The Lord was without sin. He fulfilled the requirements of the Mosaic Law. Therefore He was able to offer Himself as our atonement.

We are not automatically covered, and thereby protected, from God the Father's justice. Faith must compel us to cry out to the Lord to forgive and to cover us. Only then are we fit to stand before Him. How beautiful is Galatians 3:26-27. 'You are all sons of God through faith in Christ Jesus, for all of you who were baptised into Christ have clothed yourselves with Christ.'

Reflection: I would like to thank you, Lord, for clothing me in Christ's righteousness!

The Cosmic conflict of Passover

Day 3

Key verse: *The blood will be a sign for you on the houses where you are; and when I see the blood, I will pass over you. No destructive plague will touch you when I strike Egypt. Exodus 12:13.*

The lamb was slain. The lintels and doorposts of the houses were stained by blood. Israel huddled inside. A roast lamb was their meal and they were dressed ready to move at the command of Moses. That night was to be the culmination of the contest between the God of Israel and the idols of Egypt. 'On that same night I will pass through Egypt and strike down every firstborn–both men and animals–and *I will bring judgment on all the gods of Egypt. I am the Lord'*. (Exodus 12:12. emphasis added). The cosmic conflict which surrounded the first Passover is made plain.

Centuries later, in an upper room on the eve of another Passover, the meaning of the first Passover was summed up. Jesus applied it to Himself as the Lamb of God. In Him would be fulfilled all the spiritual implications infusing this event. This must have been a momentous, even faith shaking, concept. The disciples believed the very traditions in which they had been raised. Now Jesus was reshaping those hallowed teachings and practices.

We should not downplay their confusion. It would have appeared to them that their world was falling apart. Jesus had also talked about betrayal and death, which seems to have deafened the disciples to the fact of victory (Read John 13-14). After the cross and resurrection they would begin to understand.

Jesus knew the approaching cross involved more than dealing with humanity's sin. There was to be a battle of the light against darkness, the demonic against the Son of Man, the Lord God's grace against the enslaving guilt of Satan. The cross was to become the final battle for spiritual, moral, eternal sovereignty. When Christ's cross appeared in history, it would make its claim for the allegiance of men and women.

In the three hours of darkness as Jesus was on the cross the demonic forces entered into the fray. If it wasn't for some of the apostolic letters we would never have known this aspect of our Salvation. 'Christ...disarmed the powers and authorities, he made a public spectacle of them, triumphing over them by the cross' (Colossians 2:13-15). Is it any wonder the forces of darkness hate the message of the Cross. It is the never ending story of their defeat, humiliation and ultimate destiny.

Does this mean they sulk and leave us alone?

No!

They know about our salvation, but want to make us miserable disciples, faithless witnesses, insipid pray-ers and stingy stewards. Will a believer in the Lord Jesus be able to stand against a sustained attack of doubt, blackmail, fear and threats? If so, how?

Romans 8:38-39 provides our assurance: 'I am convinced that neither death nor life, neither angels nor demons, neither the present nor the future, nor any powers, neither heights nor depths, nor anything else in all creation, will be able to separate us from the love of God that is in Christ Jesus our Lord.'

We still have to wrestle against their evil intentions, but not in our own strength. We have the Sword of the Spirit and the Armour of Christ which renders the demonic attack unsuccessful (Ephesians 6:10-18).

Reflection: Every time I celebrate the Lord's Supper, every time I mention the cross, every time I talk about Calvary, I celebrate Christ's victory. What a privilege!

Strange Glory

Day 4

Key verses: *The hour has come for the Son of Man to be glorified. John 12:23. Father, glorify your name. John 12:28.*

Glory should conjure up in our minds radiance from beauty, brilliance from power, ecstasy from fame. The exact opposite is mirrored in ugliness, powerlessness and shame.

Glory is associated intimately with God within the pages of Scripture. Psalm 29 is devoted to the theme of God's glory. Verse two says: 'Ascribe to the Lord the glory due to his name; worship the Lord in the splendour of his holiness.'

How then is it possible to understand what Jesus said in John 12:23. 'The hour has come for the Son of Man to be glorified.' This wasn't about His glory in creation, or His power in miracles. It related to His coming ignoble death.

His countrymen considered Him a blasphemer. The Romans viewed Him as a terrorist. Where is the radiance of beauty in the cross? Where is the power of a crucified man? Where is the ecstasy of joy in being brutalised? Unless something dramatic and humanly impossible takes place to transform such horror, the crucified one is forever cursed.

Why is it that you and I glory in the crucified One?

Because of the voice from Heaven after Jesus cried out, 'Father, glorify your name!' The reply was, 'I have glorified it, and will glorify it again.' (John 12:28). What was about to happen at Golgotha was to become the most amazing demonstration of glory, ever!

Why is that possible?

Because it fulfils prophecy recorded in the thirty-nine books of the Old Testament. From the symbolism of Abraham and Isaac in Genesis 22 and Psalm 22's graphic description of a crucifixion combined with Isaiah 53's theology of substitution and redemption the reader stands awestruck.

Jesus endured sordid, degraded and satanic depths beyond our imagination to offer men and women a way of escape. There is also a second aspect involved in 'and (I) will glorify it again.' This promise incorporates the power of the resurrection. It verifies the person and achievement of Jesus as the Christ. Even in this chapter of John the resurrection is implied. 'Whoever serves me must follow me; and where I am, my servant also will be.'

There isn't much incentive for us to follow Jesus if it simply ends in the grave. Rather, in John 17:24, Jesus prays that His disciples will be with Him and see His glory. Doesn't that thrill your heart and make the difficulties of the Christian life pale into insignificance?

In harmony with such a hope is the fruitfulness of the Gospel becoming evident in the lives of believers. When you responded to Jesus you proved the point of what He was emphasising. You are the fruit of His humiliation, suffering and resurrection. You have and are declaring that Jesus is Lord and Saviour.

You are also a testimony that, through the offence of the Cross, a platform for reconciliation between you and God was established. 'Therefore, if anyone is in Christ, he is a new creation; the old has gone, the new has come! All this is from God, who reconciled us to himself through Christ and gave us the ministry of reconciliation' (2 Corinthians 5:17-19).

Reflection: As the Lord God brought glory out of the cross, rejoice in the promise of what He will do in your life in time and eternity.

Lifted Up

Day 5

Key verse:: *Just as Moses lifted up the snake in the desert, so the Son of Man must be lifted up John 3:14.*

Do you sense the imperative? What is the compulsion motivating the '*must*'?

In Numbers 21:4-9 the people grumble against God, His power and His character. He could not allow this to go uncontested. The invasion of the serpents and their deadly bite causes them to cry out to God for forgiveness. Through the bronze snake God provided a visible expression of grace. However, a person had to lift up his eyes to it before it was effective. Faith must lock onto God's grace to be effective!

Jesus interpreted the story for Nicodemus. It was about the Son of Man who would fulfil the symbolism portrayed. No better description can be found than Paul's to the Corinthian church. 'God made him who had no sin to be sin for us, so that in him we might become the righteousness of God' (2 Corinthians 5:21).

What happened at Calvary was historical, prominent and verifiable. It compelled people to look. It still does! What happens after that is a heart matter. You and I have had to face the grim reality of our rebellion against God's character and word. We have been told the One on the cross was taking our place, our judgement, our punishment. Do we believe it?

'*Jesus said, when you have lifted up the Son of Man, then you will know that I am the one I claim to be...*' *(John 8:28).*

Once again notice the imperative! This time it is '*when*'.

The Lord was under no illusions concerning His destiny. He knew His hour was approaching. What Jesus said to the twelve at Caesarea Philippi of His suffering, death and resurrection was about to happen. When He was lifted up, what He had taught, what He had done and what had been spoken about at His birth would, or should, become clear and understandable.

How?

Through the nation's very scriptures coming alive with meaning! These scriptures were and are the foundation for understanding Jesus and His mission.

'Now is the time for judgment on this world; now the prince of this world will be driven out. But I, when I am lifted up from the earth, will draw all men to myself' John 12:31-32.

Here again is an imperative!

'I will draw' speaks of the power of the lifting up of Jesus. It doesn't say everyone who is drawn to Him responds in a positive, faith submitting, life changing way. It is highlighting the fact that no one can ignore or resist an appointment arranged by the Holy Spirit. The purpose of the meeting is to make a decision about who Jesus is. Faith makes Him Saviour. Unbelief makes Him Judge.

Words are interesting in their uses and the pictures they paint in the mind. This is true of the Greek word for *'lifted up'*. It has the meaning of being hauled up as onto the cross, it also means to be exalted by being placed upon a throne.

How beautifully these two pictures combine in the person of Jesus.

Reflection: What excites me most about the three passages describing the lifting up of Jesus?

Now is the Hour

Day 6

Key verse: *Now my heart is troubled, and what shall I say? Father, save me from this hour? No, it was for this very reason I came to this hour. John 12:27.*

Heaven's clock is precise. When scripture mentions a time frame it means what it says. Satan may seek to prevent it; the World may try and delay it; unbelievers can deny it; but scripture highlights it. Consider the following records. God spoke to Abraham about his offspring serving four hundred years in a foreign land as slaves. The fulfilment is recorded in Exodus 12:40-41. It mentions four hundred and thirty years, the extra thirty are before the Pharaoh who didn't know Joseph appeared on the scene. Jeremiah spoke of seventy years captivity and wrote it down. Later, Daniel read it. In Daniel 9 he calls on the Lord to honour Jeremiah's prophecy. God did! Jesus likened what was to happen to Him to Jonah's three days in the belly of the giant fish.

This may help us to understand Jesus' awareness when He consistently insisted His hour was not yet. The Gospel of John highlights a number of occasions such as at the wedding in Cana (John 2:4); when attempts were made to arrest Him (John 7:30. 8:20); then in John 12 Jesus indicates that the hour is coming upon Him (John 12:23, 27. 13:1. 17:1.).

Israel's day began as the sun set. This came from Genesis 1 where each day is classified as 'And there was evening, and there was morning'. The Passover lamb was to be slaughtered between the evenings. This would make it 2:30 pm. 3:30 pm is the time it was placed on the altar to be consumed by fire.

In Mark's gospel we have the Jewish timetable for the crucifixion. As Jesus was lifted onto the cross it was the time of the morning sacrifice – the third hour. From the sixth hour until the ninth, darkness covered God's judgement upon the one who bore our sin. The ninth hour was the usual hour for the evening sacrifice. In our time that would be around 3.00 pm. The cry of Jesus, 'It is finished', would have coincided with the completion of the Passover sacrifice in the temple.

There is no way the timing of the crucifixion could have been manipulated by human ingenuity. Through all the complexities of religious and political jousting the Lord God met His timetable. Peter's address to the crowd on Pentecost day links God's purpose and human activity. 'This man (Jesus) was handed over to you by God's set purpose and foreknowledge; and you, with the help of wicked men put him to death by nailing him to the cross' (Acts 2:23).

The first Passover was an invitation from God to trust Him. He called Israel to a journey from bondage to being His witnesses. Subsequent Passovers were to express the nation's joy in the Lord God as they remembered their past, enjoyed the present and anticipated the future with God.

Our Passover, Jesus Christ, calls upon us to a similar journey! Every time we share in communion we look back to the hour of our redemption from sin and judgement. We also look to the 'now' and declare His faithfulness. Finally we see in it a faith statement about His return to rule upon this earth in God's kingdom.

Reflection: Refresh your memory of the 'hour' you discovered Jesus as your 'Passover' from the Father's judgement upon your sin. Can you recall how you felt and what it meant to you?

By His Stripes

Day 7

Key verse: *We all, like sheep, have gone astray, and each has turned to his own way; and the Lord has laid on him the iniquity of us all. Isaiah 53:6.*

After the sacrificial lamb was slaughtered it was flayed, washed, then roasted. Every aspect was infused with spiritual meaning. The body bore the judgement on the person's sin; the blood cleansed the believer's inner realm of sin's stench and stain. The poured out life indicated propitiation, redemption, justification and peace with God.

Jesus experienced the spiritual implication of the lamb's sacrifice in reverse: He was flayed by the Roman soldiers before being nailed to the cross and then pierced. The picture Peter presents of Christ's treatment speaks of a body bloodied and bruised beyond recognition. What then, is the significance of Peter's words about the wounds of Christ or, as the King James Version puts it, 'by his stripes we are healed' (1 Peter 2:24)?

Was the apostle equating the work of scourging as an act of the great Physician? No! The sacrifice of the Son of Man is a judicial matter, not a health care issue as is sometimes used to promote faith healing. Jesus and the issues relating to the cross fulfil the tabernacle/temple sacrifices. As the blood dealt with redemption of sinners, the wounds of Christ dealt with the disobedience of those under the Davidic kingship covenant. Psalm 89:30-34: 'If his sons (David's offspring) forsake my law and do not follow my statutes, if they violate my decrees and fail to keep my commands, I will punish their sin with the rod, their iniquity with flogging; but I will not take my love from him, nor will I ever betray my faithfulness. I will not violate my covenant or alter what my lips have uttered.'

When Jesus trod the way of the cross, when He was crucified, He also died on behalf of His enemies. 'Since we have now been justified by his blood, how much more shall we be saved from God's wrath through him! For if, when we were God's enemies, we were reconciled to him through the death of his Son, how much more, having been reconciled, shall we be saved through his life!' (Romans 5:9-10).

However, what does the Lord do when judgement is required for those He calls His children? Under the Old Testament a disobedient son could face capital punishment. Escaping that, he could expect severe chastisement! The implications are relevant for us today. We are God's children through faith in Jesus Christ. The terms describing that are 'born again' or 'adoption' into God's family. We know our behaviour, our thoughts and intents of the mind are often far from pleasing to our Heavenly Father. We have our idols which seduce our worship; there are priorities which pollute our souls and treatment of family and friends unbecoming of the Name of Jesus.

If our Heavenly Father dealt with us according to our sins we would be consumed. He must, however, deal with the issue! Isaiah 53:4-5 says, 'Surely he took up our infirmities and carried our sorrows, yet we considered him stricken by God, smitten by him, and afflicted. But he was pierced for our transgressions, he was crushed for our iniquities; the punishment that brought us peace was upon him, and by his wounds we are healed.'

Peter, in his letter, equates the suffering of Christ through the flogging as providing healing between the Father and His wayward, ungrateful, ignorant children. The breach, deserving the severest punishment was borne and healed by Jesus. Yes, we will be chastised, but not destroyed (Hebrews 12:5-12).

How could all this be accomplished? Peter refers to Jesus as the Chief Shepherd, therefore we are His flock. However, Jesus didn't suffer for our sins as the Shepherd. He did that as The Lamb of God. That means He became one of us and that specifically to be the sacrificial lamb.

Here is the awesome wonder of Grace. Jesus experienced the savagery of the 'wolves', the cruelty of false shepherds and the hatred of the powers of darkness. As the Lamb of God Jesus faced all that plus the burden of our sins and failures and won. Having triumphed as the Lamb that brought salvation in all its shades of meaning to fulfilment, He has become, once again, our Chief Shepherd.

Reflection: Write a prayer of thanksgiving addressed to God the Father for what Jesus means to you. From time to time look at it and see how your love for Jesus has grown.

The Blood of the Covenant
Day 8

Key verse: *The life of the creature is in the blood, and I have given it to you to make atonement for yourselves on the altar; it is the blood that makes atonement for one's life. Leviticus 17:11.*

The spear of the soldier penetrated the side of Jesus, who was already dead. Out flowed blood and water according to John's account as an eye witness (John 19:34). The fulfilment of the temple sacrificial system was now complete. For as the blood streamed out it was a statement about the life of Jesus! It had been shed. This was important for the fulfilment of the Old Covenant's symbolism. The scripture which says, 'Without the shedding of blood, (the poured out life) there is no remission of sin' was now accomplished.

In the original Passover in Exodus 12 the blood on the lintel and door posts of the house told an important story. The inhabitants were protected by the life of the lamb surrendered in death. When it speaks of Jesus being our Passover (1 Corinthians 5:7) it is teaching us that we are protected by His life, which was surrendered to death. His surrendered life becomes our hiding place from Judgement.

Whenever we read in the scriptures about the blood of Christ it refers to His life given rather than taken. There is more to the term than mere death, for it speaks of an offering, a substitution, an atonement! When Christ's blood flowed He was collecting our sin's wages. At the same time He was offering us the gift of life (Romans 6:23).

Christ's life is the centre point of our faith, hope, love and assurance. His earthly life, lived out under the strictest of examination, passed the test for sinlessness. His poured out life satisfied all the symbols of Israel's sacrificial system.

This was verified by the resurrection. His risen life is our only hope of being accepted by the Father and able to enjoy Heaven's atmosphere. Perhaps we can understand a little more what Paul meant when he said, 'God... made us alive with Christ even when we were dead in transgressions—it is by grace you have been saved. And God raised us up with Christ and seated us with him in the heavenly realms in Christ Jesus...' (Ephesians 2:4-6).

What has Jesus Christ secured for us by His poured out life? 'Since we have now been justified by his blood, how much more shall we be saved from God's wrath through him' (Romans 5:9). Justified is a legal term which means to be pardoned. The price has been paid. Jesus took God the Father's anger towards us. He has reconciled us by His shed blood.

'In him we have redemption through his blood, the forgiveness of sins...' (Ephesians 1:7). We were slaves to sin, captives to death, caught in the kingdom of darkness. Now in Jesus Christ we have been set free and have been forgiven. Praise the Lord for the price is paid! More than that, our Lord has purged us, cleansed us from sin and continues to cleanse us when we foul our high calling. (1 John 1:7-9).

The word 'holy' or 'sanctify' holds the idea of being set aside for God's purposes. God wants us to be co-labourers with Him in achieving His purposes. He makes us holy for this reason, otherwise we would be not much more than a tool. Hebrews 13:12 tells us we have been made holy through the blood of Christ.

Those God appoints to oversee his work must not only cherish the privilege, but tremble at the responsibility. Why? 'Be shepherds of the church of God, which he bought with his own blood' (Acts 20:28). That's why!

The Old Covenant led to Jesus Christ. Every sacrifice pointed to Calvary. Every associated promise was to be released in its fullness through the shed blood of Jesus. We do not dwell upon the blood as merely haemoglobin. In fact it was His very life poured out. So we can say 'Amen' to Hebrews 13:20-21: 'May the God of peace, who through the blood of the eternal covenant brought back from the dead our Lord Jesus Christ, that great Shepherd of the sheep, equip you with everything good for doing his will ...'.

Reflection: Are there any new dimensions to your understanding about the blood of Christ shed for you? Have you been refreshed in what you previously understood?

Father Forgive them
Day 9

Key verse: *Jesus said, Father, forgive them, for they do not know what they are doing. Luke 26:34.*

Why did Jesus say this?

He understood the intent of the national leadership. They had planned to get rid of Him. He was disturbing the people with ideas of God's coming kingdom. That was dangerous and a threat to their position because of the Roman occupation. John 11:49-50 records Caiaphas the high priest as saying, 'You do not realise that it is better for you that one man die for the people than that the whole nation perish.' Their conspiracy to frame Jesus and hand Him over to the Romans for execution was a well orchestrated judicial murder.

Why, then, did Jesus pray they be forgiven?

Under Mosaic Law a murderer was to be shown no pity. He was to be punished, a life for a life. This was to prevent the land from being polluted by the unpunished shedding of innocent blood. If someone was killed accidentally there was provision for him from the avenger of blood. The offender could run to one of six cities of Refuge and plead his case before the elders. Having his plea accepted gave him protection as long as he stayed in that city for the length of the high priest's life.

What was the purpose motivating this prayer?

He turned their pre-meditated murder into unintentional manslaughter because of their ignorance and unbelief. Under the Mosaic sacrificial system there was provision for the sins of ignorance. 'If a person sins and does what is forbidden in any of the Lord's commands, even though he does not know it he is guilty and will be held responsible. He is to bring to the priest as a guilt offering a ram from the flock, one without defect and of proper value. In this way the priest will make atonement for him for the wrong he has committed unintentionally, and he will be forgiven' (Leviticus 5:17-18).

What was the result of Jesus prayer?

Everyone involved in the betrayal, abuse and misrepresentation of Jesus was covered. They had another opportunity to understand Jesus was the promised Messiah; He was the fulfilment of prophecy; He was their Passover Lamb; He was their city of refuge; He was their atonement. He was their Saviour! If Jesus hadn't prayed that prayer there would be no hope of forgiveness for those in the conspiracy.

More than that, what hope would there have been for many of us? Before our conversion we were as guilty as the Jewish leaders in betraying and crucifying the Son of Man. Our deliberate and callous intent is also covered by the Lord's prayer from the cross.

When speaking to a crowd in Jerusalem Peter reminded them of their deeds of betrayal. Then he added words of hope. 'Now, brothers, I know that you acted in ignorance, as did your leaders…Repent, then, and turn to God, so that your sins may be wiped out…' (Acts 3:17-19).

We live under that same covering. Before his conversion the Apostle Paul was a savage opponent of Christ and His Church. He systematically went about destroying those who claimed Jesus as Lord and Saviour. In his testimony Paul clings to the very essence of Jesus' prayer and the Jewish sacrifice for sins of ignorance. Writing to Timothy, he said, 'Even though I was once a blasphemer and a persecutor and a violent man, I was shown mercy because I acted in ignorance and unbelief…Here is a trustworthy saying that deserves full acceptance: Christ Jesus came into the world to save sinners – of whom I am the worst. But for that very reason I was shown mercy so that in me, the worst of sinners, Christ Jesus might display his unlimited patience as an example for those who would believe in him and receive eternal life' (1 Timothy 1:13-16).

Look at Christ on the cross from the background of the Law and statutes of Moses. You will begin to understand the completeness of Christ's death. Every facet of our rebellion and sinful behaviour is dealt with in Christ. His prayer for our forgiveness opens up a new life. The issues are no longer how bad we've been, nor how far we've wandered from God. Rather the issue concerns how we have responded to Christ Jesus' offer of mercy, grace and redemption.

Reflection: What are the implications of Jesus being both our city of refuge and our eternal High Priest?

Look and Live

Day 10

Key verse: *The Lord said to Moses, 'Make a snake and put it up on a pole; anyone who is bitten can look at it and live.' So Moses made a bronze snake and put it up on a pole. Numbers 21:5-6.*

Ridiculous!

Who thought up such a silly remedy for snake bite in the wilderness?

Reading the account in Numbers highlights the shockwaves arising from God's judgement on undisciplined, unjustified and unbecoming attitudes of the people of Israel towards God. He wasn't being vindictive. Behind His actions was a twofold purpose. The first was to awaken a sense of their need for forgiveness. The second was to point to something in the future.

The people had forgotten the reasons for their tiresome wanderings as detailed in Numbers 13 and 14. Unbelief had robbed them of entrance into the Promised Land. Hardness of heart had produced convenient spiritual amnesia. A similar blight can affect us all.

Why snakes?

Perhaps within the area they were plentiful. God may have used them as a reminder of what caused Adam and Eve to rebel. For us the reason is clear. It was to be a metaphor of a future life-giving event.

The Lord inflicted the judgment. At the same time He provided the remedy grace. The bronze snake was a symbol of their problem, a testimony to their denigration of God. It also became, through the power of grace, His cure. As it was lifted up before the gaze of the nation, it condemned and humbled them. But there was also hope. Look and live was the invitation of the Eternal One. Unbelief, self pity or hostility towards the Lord would keep the eyes lowered. Belief in the word proclaimed would draw the eyes upward with a desperate longing. As they looked, the promise of God responded. His grace penetrated the very being of the believer and made him or her whole.

Why did the people ask Moses to pray on their behalf?

They could have sought Yahweh personally. The reason would be the same as ours in similar situations. A sense of personal unworthiness mixed with a deep sense of dread. They recognised the need for a mediator. We realise the same need. 'There is one God and one mediator between God and men, the man Christ Jesus, who gave himself as a ransom for all men…' (1 Timothy 2:5-6)

What was the point of it, if indeed it had any meaning at all?

For centuries this account of Israel and the bronze snake on a pole was left as a story told but unexplained. It took a conversation between Jesus and Nicodemus to have it solved. The response of the Pharisee is not recorded. It must have made an awesome impression, as Nicodemus became a follower. On two further occasions the Lord Jesus stressed the fact of being 'lifted up.' In John 8:28 Jesus, speaking to the Jews, said 'When you have lifted up the Son of Man, then you will know that I am the one I claim to be…' In chapter 12:32 Jesus claimed that in His being lifted up, all men would be drawn to Him and the prince of this world will be driven out.

Being lifted up dealt with the poison the Serpent in Eden's Garden injected into Adam and his descendents. It isn't the historical fact that removes the poison from within. It is in the believing Jesus did it on your behalf as the Son of Man and you have looked to Him for salvation.

Reflection: The One who was lifted up for my healing from sin is also my mediator. For Jesus knew that after being cured I'd be bitten again. When that eventuates He becomes my advocate (1 John 2:1-2).

The Curtain is Torn
Day 11

Key Verse: *'Therefore, brethren, since we have confidence to enter the Most Holy Place by the blood of Jesus, by a new and living way opened for us through the curtain, that is, his body...' Hebrews 10:19-20.*

The 'curtain' is the term used here for the body of Christ. The KJV uses the word veil. The writer of Hebrews makes a strange application about the temple curtain. The temple curtain separated the Holy Place from the Holiest of Holies. The curtain stretched the whole width of the temple and from roof to floor. Behind it was the Ark of the Covenant, symbolising God's presence. It was approachable once a year, briefly and only with the blood of an animal. That day was Yom Kippur, the Day of Atonement.

When Jesus cried out in a loud voice, 'It is finished' it was, in fact, a victory shout! At that precise moment when He died, the curtain in the temple was rent from top to bottom (Matthew 27:50-51). No person could have done it. God the Father was demonstrating that His Son had achieved the otherwise impossible feat of making the unapproachable God, approachable. When you look at the temple curtain it becomes a symbol of the claim Jesus made in John 14:6: 'I am the way, and the truth and the life. No one comes to the Father except through me.'

If we had ventured into the Holy of Holies the first thing confronting us would be the Ark of the Covenant. On its top was the golden mercy seat with Cherubim at either end peering down as though seeing the contents of the Ark. In it were three items. Each one a reminder of the nation's unbelief and rebellion! These were 'the gold jar of manna, Aaron's staff that had budded, and the stone tablets of the covenant' (Hebrews 9:4). Each of these spoke of condemnation and judgement. The cherubim can almost be imagined as thinking 'how can anyone approach God with all this against them?' What could cover the symbols of failure and punishment? Only blood!

The book of Hebrews makes it clear that Jesus ascended to Glory. He entered the heavenly place of which the Tabernacle was a copy. Jesus, as the risen Son of Man and our substitute, covered the items of offence with

His own poured out life (Hebrews 9:15-26). Only when all of that had been accomplished could a person approach the presence of God. But here again we face a problem. Under the earthly worship system only a priest could enter into God's unseen, but very real, presence. And only the High Priest, properly dressed and purified, had access to the Holy of Holies.

How has God made it possible for us to enter His presence?

By making us 'a chosen people, a royal priesthood, a holy nation, a people belonging to God, that you may declare the praises of Him who called you out of darkness into His wonderful light' (1 Peter 2:9-10). In Christ we have also the proper garments for the joy and honour of entering into the throne room of the King of Kings and Lord of Lords. The importance of the proper clothing cannot be overestimated. Improper dress is offensive to God and also a barrier to our being listened to.

When we pray we often sign off 'In Jesus name' as though it is a code word or a ritual statement guaranteeing action on our petition. The name is not a tag, but our location. The name is the very nature of our Lord. Therefore to pray in His name is to be clothed in, living in, worshipping in His very being. Only then are we able to walk into the presence of our Heavenly Father in the company of our High Priest, Jesus.

All of these privileges and garments were secured for us when Jesus opened the way by His pierced body and poured out life

Reflection: Have I thanked my Lord for the significance of His being the Way, the Truth and the Life whereby He leads me into His Father's presence?

The Cup and the Cross
Day 12

Key verse: *This cup is the new covenant in my blood; do this, whenever you drink it, in remembrance of me. 1 Corinthians 11:25.*

Cups come in all shapes and sizes, but have one purpose. They hold liquid for drinking purposes. In the Scriptures a number of cups are mentioned, some literal, some symbolic. The latter ones hold potent mixtures either for judgement or blessing.

There is the cup of God's wrath. The Psalmist wrote, 'In the hand of the Lord is a cup full of foaming wine mixed with spices; He pours it out, and all the wicked of the earth drink it down to its very dregs' (Ps 75:8). It is the cup of His fury. There is something within us that is repelled by the doctrine of God getting angry. This is more often due to a false concept of God and a weak view of holiness, sin and accountability. We also fail to appreciate God doesn't like being called a liar. This happens when a person doesn't believe the testimony God has given about Jesus Christ in Scripture (1 John 5:10).

This cup of God's fury against sin in all its guises was what faced Jesus Christ at Calvary. This is why its knowledge crushed His soul in Gethsemane. His cry, 'Take this cup from me; yet not my will, but yours be done' (Luke 22:42) reveals the horror in the cup. At the same time it manifests His obedience.

In the hours of darkness which covered the conflict on the cross, Jesus drank the cup of fury. He consumed it, yet it couldn't consume Him. His victory cry, 'It is finished' also can be interpreted as meaning: 'I have drunk the cup dry!'

The psalmist talks about another cup. It is the cup most longed for, yet is second in line to be drunk. The 'cup of salvation' is the refreshing, revitalising and transforming nectar longed for by those with a thirst for God. How can they reach for it if the 'cup of wrath' must be drunk first? If anyone of us is called upon to sip, let alone consume it all, we would be eternally doomed. We would not have any life left to reach for the second cup.

When we understand the amazing mercy of Jesus in drinking the first cup for us, we should bow before Him in awestruck gratitude. Because of what He drank on the cross the quote of the psalmist can resonate from our hearts and lips: 'How can I repay the Lord for all his goodness to me? I will lift up the cup of salvation and call upon the name of the Lord. I will fulfil my vows to the Lord in the presence of all his people' (Ps 116:12-14).

The evening before His crucifixion Jesus had the famous meal with the twelve disciples. Throughout this time four cups were drunk as expressive of the Passover celebration. Two of those cups are mentioned in the gospel accounts. One was before the bread, the other followed the bread. One spoke of His blood bringing in the new covenant, the other of a future celebration in the Kingdom of God (Luke 22:14-20). This is a testimony to Jesus as the Christ, the Son of the Living God. Every time we share in the Eucharist/Lord's Supper/Holy Communion, our Saviour and Lord is remembered. The fourth cup (the second one mentioned) is the cup by which we declare we are only doing this until Jesus comes again. In our Communion time we have combined these cups.

If there is no cross or resurrection of Jesus all that awaits us is the cup of God's wrath. It cannot be emptied by personal works of merit. It cannot be siphoned out through religious rituals. It cannot be knocked out of God's hand with our self righteous 'purity'.

To drink or not to drink is not the question. The question is who will drink the contents of the first cup? The glorious Gospel of Jesus Christ said right from the beginning, 'Jesus has taken the first cup and drained it dry'. The second cup awaits the lips of faith after you claim Him Lord and Saviour. Then Christ Jesus will drink that cup in His coming kingdom with His people as He promised. It will be a drink with eternal satisfaction.

Reflection: What are some of the memories and hopes which flood our minds when we take the cup of Communion expressing our relationship with God?

The Tree

Day 13

Key verse: *Christ redeemed us from the curse of the law by becoming a curse for us, for it is written: Cursed is everyone who is hung on a tree. Galatians 3:13.*

Trees! Without trees what a desolate planet this would be! Trees are portrayed in scripture in all their glory and with dramatic, spiritual implications. From Genesis 1 through to Revelation 22 trees play a significant role in human destiny.

In the Garden of Eden stood two special trees! One was the Tree of Life, the other the Tree of the Knowledge of good and evil. Adam was under orders not to eat of the tree of good and evil for the result would be death. The story is known; the cost seen every moment of every day since. In the Genesis account cherubim with a flaming sword unsheathed guarded the tree of life. Would there ever be a time in history when the swords were sheathed and the way to the tree of life be thrown open?

Another tree is mentioned in Deuteronomy 21:22: 'If any man guilty of a capital offence is put to death and his body is hung on a tree, you must not leave his body on the tree overnight. Be sure to bury him that same day, because anyone who is hung on a tree is under God's curse.' The Mosaic Law stipulated the punishment for a capital offence was stoning. The idea behind placing the body on a tree, or stake, was to act as a warning. It would also express the law's severity.

Let the centuries roll on until the time of Jesus Christ. Israel was under Roman occupation. Rome alone had the right of execution and we read about the Sanhedrin demanding of Pilate the death sentence for Jesus. The Jewish charges were about blasphemy. The Roman law considered Him a threat to Caesar. Jesus couldn't be stoned but he was crucified on what the Jewish people would term 'a tree'. It's in these seemingly incidental features of Scripture we can see the foreknowledge and fingerprint of God.

The term cross is used by Paul to the Gentiles but to the Jewish believers in Galatia he uses the term 'tree'. Notice how Paul applied the crucifixion to the account in Deuteronomy. 'Christ redeemed us from the curse of the law by becoming a curse for us, for it is written, "Cursed is everyone who is hung on a tree". He redeemed us in order that the blessing given to Abraham might come to the Gentiles through Christ Jesus, so that by faith we might receive the promise of the Spirit' (Galatians 3:13-14). Jesus was cursed by the Mosaic Law. If He was guilty as charged there isn't anyway He could rise again. The resurrection as foretold declared Heaven's verdict, – not guilty! What Jesus did achieve by being cursed was to rob the law of its judicial power of death over men and women. Peter explained it, 'He (Jesus) himself bore our sins in his body on the tree, so that we might die to sins and live for righteousness; by his stripes we are healed' (1 Peter 2:24).

What implications does all this have for us?

When Jesus removed the curse, paid the penalty for Adam's treason, plus the sin of the whole world, the way to the tree of life was opened. In effect the cherubim sheathed their swords. A miracle of grace took place at the cursed tree. The Almighty God turned a curse into a blessing.

We come across the tree of life in Revelation 2:7. The specific reference is to the church in Ephesus. Its overflow, however, reaches to us. 'He who has an ear, let him hear what the Spirit says to the churches. To him who overcomes, I will give the right to eat from the Tree of life, which is in the paradise of God.

We cannot expect to enjoy the Tree of life's fruit until we have been to the cursed tree. There our unbelief and rebellion is dealt with. In essence, when we confess our need of Jesus as Saviour He delivers us from the curse. When we declare Him as our Lord we are embracing the Tree of life. Throughout the gospel of John the term 'life' in all its nuances is wrapped up in Jesus.

I love being under His 'branches'! What about you?

Reflection: Hebrews 12:2 mentions Jesus despising the shame of the cross. As I think about that in the light of the cursed tree, what comes to my mind?

The Triumph of the Cross
Day 14

Key verse: *Having disarmed the powers and authorities, he made a public spectacle of them, triumphing over them by the cross. Colossians 2:15.*

The young man sat at his desk. It was the first week of Bible College and he was wrestling with his past. It was as though the devil was in the room accusing him of hypocrisy, carnality and shallowness, and he was right. Conscience was aroused, projecting images of the past, suggesting he wasn't worthy to be a minister. Desperate, the student flicked open the Bible and his eyes fell upon 'God made you alive with Christ. He forgave us all our sins, having cancelled the written code, with its regulations, that was against us and stood opposed to us; he took it away, nailing it to the cross.'

Claiming that scripture gave the young man immediate relief! The conscience was silenced, Satan's accusations, true in themselves, were stamped 'paid' and cancelled. Once again, the all encompassing power of the cross dealt with issues of the heart, the past, and an aroused conscience.

Our conscience seems to be able to store our yesterdays with all their errors. Then it often throws them into our mind at most inconvenient moments. We believe God has blotted out of His sight our confessed sins but our memory won't forget. When our failures appear in our mind do we have a delete button? '…the blood of Christ, who through the eternal Spirit offered himself unblemished to God, cleanse(d) our conscience from acts that lead to death, so that we may serve the living God' (Hebrews9:14). We may have our consciences aroused about the past but we can silence them. This comes about through praising the Lord Jesus for His triumph in our life and the cleansing He has provided.

In the Gospels it says the devil left off testing Jesus for a while, probably a very short time. When we were thinking of becoming Christians the devil came down hard on us to try and prevent it. Our confessing Christ as Saviour and Lord enrages the devil. He makes use of every opportunity to remind us of our pre-Christian life. His aim is to render us impotent in faithfulness and determination. The purpose is to corrupt our testimony to the indwelling presence and power of Jesus.

The devil doesn't have to lie. He has his dossier on us and brings it to bear on our minds so as to crush and blackmail. Paul had reminded the readers in Colossians 1:21 'Once you were alienated from God and were enemies in your mind because of your evil behaviour'. There is only one answer capable of silencing Satan's clamour for God's death penalty. It is the cross! But the cross wasn't going to carry them or us. It would hold Jesus, our substitute. 'But now he has reconciled you by Christ's physical body through death to present you holy in his sight, without blemish and free from accusation' (Colossians 1:22).

The passage in Colossians 2:13-15 is marvellous in its grace statement, in its promise and in its victory. All the accusations of our offences against God and His commands were nailed to the cross in the person of Jesus, the Son of Man. All our open and hidden moral corruption was recorded and hammered onto the cross. Pilate wrote a sign and placed it on the Cross. It said Jesus, King of the Jews. That was visible. There could have been an invisible sign posted on the cross and visible to heaven and hades. It might have said, 'The law's debt paid in full. The broken code and violated regulations are cancelled, paid for, removed forever.' Praise the Lord there is freedom from the bondage of the past. Praise the Lord there is an answer to a burdened conscience. Praise the Lord there is the authority in Jesus' name to tell Satan he has nothing on us.

It is no surprise, therefore, why Satan and the forces of darkness hate the cross. *Every time* he hears it he is reminded of his defeat. *Every time* someone believes the message of Christ and Calvary the kingdom of darkness is plundered. *Every time* we sing and celebrate the message of the cross Satan is made a public spectacle, humiliated and defeated, his final doom proclaimed.

Reflection: If there are any reasons you feel Satan's accusations or you have an uneasy conscience, take it to Jesus Christ your Advocate. He will sort it out because He has already paid the price and cancelled the condemnation.

Co-Crucified

Date 15

Key verse: *For as in Adam all die, so in Christ all will be made alive. 1 Corinthians 15:22*

If you want to become a citizen of a country, other than the one you were born into, certain procedures must take place. You must make the choice. You are required to undergo a suitability examination. Then there is a time lapse between application and acceptance. After approval there is a ceremony in which you promise allegiance to your new country.

We were born into the spiritual country of Death. The Federal Head of this was Adam who consigned all his descendants to live in this world. Its features are a sin nature, corruption, decay, evil and apathy or hostility towards God the Creator. This world is very religious in a self-righteous or Satan-dominated way. The citizens of Death's country, however, sense, deep within, that there is more to existence than what is apparent. Such an inner awareness is the residue of what Adam lost when he disobeyed God. Read Genesis chapters 1-3.

The Lord God Almighty, the Creator, 'invaded' the world of Adam's creation. Hebrews 1:1-2: 'In the past God spoke to our forefathers through the prophets at many times and in various ways, but in these last days he has spoken to us by his Son, whom he appointed heir of all things, and through whom he made the universe:' Why would the Godhead, Father, Son and Holy Spirit, bother? Love's mercy with Grace's generosity wanted to provide an alternate spiritual country. This would be open to those with a heart similar to Abraham. 'He was looking forward to the city with foundations, whose architect and builder is God' (Hebrews 11:10).

How can those longing hearts find a new country in which righteousness, love, grace, forgiveness and meaning abound? This is the charter of the Gospel. This is one of the purposes of the Cross. This is the invitation of Christ to come join Him, make Him your spiritual Federal Head. The key word of His kingdom is 'Life'. 'For if, by the trespass of the one man, death reigned through that one man, how much more will those who receive God's abundant provision of grace and the gift of righteousness reign in life through the one man, Jesus Christ' (Romans 5:17).

What needs to be done by you to leave the spiritual headship of Adam and place yourself under the headship of Jesus Christ? The requirement for Christ's kingdom is resurrection life. This, of course, means you have to die. Then you need the power to come to life again as a new person. That is humanly impossible, for our sin and the Father's judgement would preclude us from rising again. Once more the wonder of Christ's power, grace and provision are displayed. On Golgotha's hill Jesus was framed by two thieves. Unseen by the human eye others were also crucified with Jesus.

Romans chapter six is a magnificent passage on that experience. There is the depiction of what took place in the spiritual realm. When you believed in and confessed Jesus as Lord and Saviour you shared in the cross of Christ Jesus. 'We know that our old self was crucified with him so that the body of sin might be done away with ... because anyone who died has been freed from sin' (Romans 6:6-7). He also paints the picture of believers going into the tomb dead with Christ. When He rose from the dead so did they! What does Paul use as the dramatic portrayal of changing countries? Not simply faith or worship, important imperatives as they are. It is Christian baptism in the manner of the New Testament, immersion in water. Peter writes '... this water symbolises baptism that now saves you also, not the removal of dirt from the body, but the pledge of a good conscience towards God. It saves you by the resurrection of Jesus Christ' (1 Peter 3:21).

That new life is in a new spiritual country. To the Lord of that realm we owe our allegiance. Our time in this world of Death is to be Christ's lights, witnesses, heralds and servants.

Reflection: As a citizen of Christ's country I'm an ambassador for Jesus Christ in the places of my appointments. What does that mean?

How God Accepts
Day 16

Key verse: *Now in Christ Jesus you who once were far away have been brought near through the blood of Christ. Ephesians 2:13.*

The gavel came down hard. The sentence was pronounced 'Guilty as charged!' The accused was in debt to the law. The penalty had to be paid. When it was paid he was free but his crime was listed for all time and for all to see.

The Bible declares 'the wages of sin is death' (Romans 6:23). The Law of the Universe is impartial and just. The physical expression of death symbolises a far deeper, eternal, spiritual death. The trouble arises in the fact that, whilst we all die and satisfy the law's demand, heaven's doors remain shut. Why? Heaven is the realm of the debt free, resurrected ones. Even in death the charges against us remain. We are powerless to rise from death's grip. God the Father, Son and Holy Spirit is unable to receive the lifeless person. To those who have written over them, 'Penalty paid. Resurrection power received. Acceptance is assured.

How, then, can you and I know for sure our debt has been paid and we have received resurrection life? Here is one of the great wonders and mysteries of the cross. Our debt is paid. In God the Judge's sight the charges against us are pardoned. Our eternal state of death is overturned. Our spirits are invested with resurrection life. After our physical death we're encompassed by a new eternal body. Read the following passages and as you do offer to God the Father a song of gratitude for Jesus and Calvary.

'I've been crucified with Christ and I no longer live, but Christ lives in me. The life I live in the body, I live by faith in the Son of God, who loved me and gave himself for me' (Galatians 2:20).

'Don't you know that all of us who were baptised into Christ Jesus were baptised into his death? We were therefore buried with him through baptism into death in order that, just as Christ was raised from the dead through the glory of the Father, we too may live a new life' (Romans 6:2-4).

What then is this new indwelling life? It is resurrection life!

We didn't manufacture it. We didn't earn it. We didn't inherit it. It was given to us. How? When we called upon the crucified and risen Lord to save us, cleanse us, remove from us the shame of the Law's pronouncements. How? Through a beautiful legal term – justification!

What does it mean?

It is a declaration that yours and my offences and falling short of God's glory have been paid. Not by you or me, but by the only One righteous enough to pay the price. It doesn't make you innocent. It declares you are pardoned. More than that, it opens the way for all the bounty of God to flow into our lives! God could have pardoned us in Christ but kept us at arm's length. He could have simply set us adrift to have another go at the impossible life. The grace of God is awe inspiring. He pardons (justifies) and cleanses us from all defilement, clothes us in Christ's righteousness and embraces us as His redeemed children. Still this wouldn't be enough for us to enjoy heaven. We require a new indwelling, eternal, resurrection life. 'Since, then, you have been raised with Christ, set your hearts on things above, where Christ is seated at the right hand of God…For you died, and your life is now hidden with Christ in God. When Christ, who is your life appears, then you also will appear with him in glory' (Colossians 3:1-4).

Do you see the total package of the cross for your salvation and acceptance into glory? From beginning to end it is all of Jesus and His achievements verified by the resurrection. Far from making us puppets this knowledge creates a celebration of worship and a life of gratitude. The apostle Peter, when writing to a persecuted fellowship, encouraged them to look beyond what oppressed them and see the promised glory. That glory rested simply and solely on the person of Jesus Christ! 'Praise be to the God and Father of our Lord Jesus Christ! In his great mercy he has given us new birth into a living hope through the resurrection of Jesus Christ from the dead, and into an inheritance that can never perish, spoil or fade–kept in heaven for you…' (I Peter 1:3-4).

Reflection: Can I think of other aspects of being justified by faith in Christ? Perhaps looking through a Bible concordance will help you discover them.

The Cross begins our Journey
Day 17

Key verse: *Dear friends, I urge you, as aliens and strangers in the world, to abstain from sinful desires, which war against your soul. Live such good lives among the pagan that, though they accuse you of doing wrong, they may see your good deeds and glorify God on the day he visits us. 1 Peter 2:11-12.*

They had it good, so good, in fact, they forgot their inheritance. Four hundred and thirty years had passed since Israel had sought drought relief in Egypt. Why worry about a promise God gave to Abraham, Isaac and Jacob? Their descendents were quite comfortable in a strange land and saw no need to look any further. Affluence is the greatest threat to seeking our true inheritance. Being comfortable dulls the sense of need. The trinkets of success divert our attention from the unfading wealth of the Kingdom of God.

Pharaoh came onto the scene and made Israel aware of their real status. They were slaves. What they possessed could easily be taken. For humankind life has many 'Pharaohs' who enjoy enslaving, corrupting and blinding people from knowing their true destiny. Behind each 'Pharaoh' stands the god of this world (2 Corinthian 4:4).

The story of the ten plagues makes it apparent Moses wasn't trying to impress. He was merely Yahweh's representative. His message: 'Let the descendents of Abraham go!' It was time to inherit the promise. Judgement was declared but God provided a safe haven for all who took His word seriously. The safe haven would be in the dwellings of those who splattered the blood of the lamb on the lintel and door-posts. Their security was the blood of the substitute lamb. The Bible declares that a person's and a creature's life is in his/her blood. It was to be the poured out life of the substitute lamb on the door which would offer security. Faith heeded. Unbelief scoffed.

The clear, precise and encompassing directions from Moses to the people relied upon the faithfulness of God's word. That hasn't changed. We are dependent upon God remaining faithful to His Word. Centuries later, in the midst of heartbreak, Jeremiah held onto God being faithful to fulfil His word as given to Abraham. 'Because of the Lord's great love we are not consumed, for his compassions never fail. They are new every morning; great is your faithfulness' (Lamentations 3:22, compare Jeremiah 32:37). In the challenges of our experiences we too are called upon to cling to the trustworthiness of God's word.

Jesus is our Passover. The implications of this are deep and wide. He took on the gods and idols of this world as the Lamb. His blood, the life poured out at Calvary, stands between the believer and God's judgement, between the believer and enslavement by the powers of Darkness, between the believer's sin, the devil's accusations and our forgiveness. 'He (Jesus) has rescued us from the dominion of darkness and brought us into the kingdom of the Son He loves (Colossians 1:13).

The historical Passover not only redeemed from bondage, it created a pilgrim people moving towards a promised land. It was an orderly exodus. To read the account is to be amazed at the logistics behind the journey. Also mentioned in this account is the change of heart by Pharaoh. He sought to recapture the redeemed nation. The spiritual truth of that is evident in the lives of the disciples of Christ today. A personal faith in the risen Lord Jesus brings the believer into a journey to his/her heavenly destination, as Philippians 3:20-21 assures us. Satan and his idols have been beaten by the cross. He, however, still seeks to pursue us as Pharaoh did to Israel. He cannot undo what Christ has achieved. His intent is to rob us of our joy, blind our eyes to our calling, breed hypocrisy in our soul and make us 'campers' instead of pilgrims.

The nation of Israel followed the pillar of fire at night and the pillar of cloud during the day. That was the visible testimony of God's presence as they journeyed. For us, we are called to follow Christ, banking on His promise to lead us and never forsake us.

What is our assurance?

It is the Holy Spirit's indwelling and His spiritual 'GPS', God's Powerful Scriptures, which will lead us to be with Jesus Christ in glory!

Reflection: As an old song put it, 'this world is not my home I'm just a passing through.'

However, what imprint am I leaving for others to follow?

Something for God the Father

Day 18

Key verse: *The Lord said to Moses, Give this command to the Israelites and say to them: See that you present to me at the appointed time the food for my offerings made by fire, as an aroma pleasing to me. Numbers 28:1-2.*

At Christmas time or birthdays there are advertisements offering something special for the person who has everything. Such people do make things difficult in the gift department. However, the same principle applies between each of us and our Heavenly Father. What can we give Him as a gift?

A clue is woven within the key verse. Every reference to the sacrificial offerings of the Tabernacle found their fulfilment in Christ. They were shadows. Jesus is the reality. Each day there were two special offerings specifically set aside for God's pleasure. The others dealt with matters covering our redemption, sanctification and relationships. Each morning and evening a sacrifice was made to begin and end the day. There is something different about them. Symbolically, it was as if the priest was lifting up to the Father the One in whom He delighted, His only Begotten, Jesus!

In Numbers 28 the emphasis of the sacrifice is for the enjoyment of God. It is 'my offering' and it is 'an aroma pleasing to the Lord'. It begins and concludes the worship and the work of the day. This was required everyday all year. It is unending. What the priest on the other side of the cross was offering by faith was for the Father's pleasure. This side of the cross when we offer our sacrifice of praise about Jesus, it is music to the Father's 'ears'.

We need to remind ourselves that the idea of sacrifice involves costs. The people of the Old Testament gave of their best animals or crops. What cost is involved when we come praising the Lord in the beauty of holiness and by the grace of Jesus? Could it be the cost of thanking God for Jesus in the midst of personal sorrow? Could it be upholding the honour of the Lord surrounded by those who profane His name? Maybe it is in submission to His will which cuts across personal ambition or replaces a cherished dream! To still love the Lord and offer thanksgiving to His Father is the price Faith offers to Love. Together they celebrate the wonder of knowing Jesus.

What is it that pleases and honours the Father most?

In His own words, 'This is my Son, whom I love; with him I am well pleased' (Matthew 3:17). At the mount of transfiguration in Matthew 17: 5 the Father says, 'This is my Son, whom I love; with him I am well pleased. Listen to him.' As Jesus drew near to the cross He called on His Father, saying, 'Father, glorify your name!' While surrounded by people, a voice from heaven replied, 'I have glorified it, and will glorify it again' (John 12:28.). In his humanity Jesus lived out His life in obedience to the will of the Father. The name above every name delights God the Father. He rejoices to hear it proclaimed and praised by those who have believed on Him.

To enter the presence of our Heavenly Father we know we are only acceptable because of our faith relationship with Jesus. To express that reality keeps us from kidding ourselves about how important we are to God. Jesus and Jesus only is our boast! Why does the writer of Hebrews tell us we can enter boldly into the throne room of heaven? Simply because Jesus walks with us, stands with us, puts a word in for us, and, it may be said, takes our spoken and unspoken words and clothes them in His authority.The gift we can offer our Heavenly Father continually is to love His Son, accept the Son's ministry and to honour Him.

Reflection: At this moment what impresses me most about Jesus and His dealings with me? How would I express that to my Heavenly Father?

The Cross and 'The Stone'

Day 19

Key verse: *The stone the builders rejected has become the capstone. Psalm 118:22.*

Jesus has some fascinating titles. Some of the ones in the Old Testament are obscure until applied by the New Testament writers. To call Jesus 'the stone' seems strange to our ears, but is full of meaning.

In Isaiah the Lord God describes Himself as a rock that causes people to stumble and fall. He also said He wanted to be a sanctuary for them. What causes people to stumble rather than find a safe place? Unbelief and disobedience sums up the problem.

In Psalm 118, widely recognised as Messianic, the writer says, 'The stone the builders rejected has become the capstone; the Lord has done this, and it is marvellous in our eyes. This is the day the Lord has made; let us rejoice and be glad in it.' Jesus quoted this passage around the meal table before going to Gethsemane. Observe the confidence in the words. Notice the One who is the creator of the events of the day, it wasn't Israel. It wasn't Rome. It wasn't the devil. God the Father orchestrated it! The cross was to carry the 'Stone' who would either become a person's sanctuary or stumbling stone.

Throughout His teaching ministry Jesus forewarned the nation about an event which would be to them a blessing or a curse. In the parable of the tenants in Mark 12 the Rabbi from Nazareth spells out how He would be treated. Once again, the passage from Isaiah is quoted. The owner of the vineyard ultimately sends his son to collect its fruit. The tenants imagine that by killing the son they could be masters of the property. The hearers grasped the implications in regard to the nation and this Jesus. Their desire to destroy Him then and there wasn't possible. They had to wait for the right time. When Jesus quoted Isaiah it was as a warning more than a threat. He had no pleasure in seeing His opponents crushed. He was preparing them for the resurrection event. They should be able to recognise what had happened and cry out to Him for mercy.

This theme is Peter's plea in Acts 4:10-12. As the Lord's spokesman he reminds them about the rejected stone being heaven's choice of the capstone. Then Peter informs the people there is no other name under heaven given for the salvation (could we say, sanctuary) of men and women. Today we are faced with a similar dilemma. If anyone accepts Jesus as naïve, nice, noble, unbalanced about being Messiah and Son of God, they are rejecting Him. Any individual who considers Jesus as the Gospels proclaim Him to be will make Him the foundation, capstone, and sanctuary of his or her life.

Why was it necessary for 'the Stone' to be subjected to such a cruel trial? Look on it as heaven's quality assurance pressure test! Was it strong enough to bear the moral and spiritual requirements to be the Messiah? Could 'the Stone' endure the moral and spiritual quicksand of earth without being sucked under? Any flaws in personality, any weakness undetected by human eyes, any fractures of spiritual integrity would emerge under the pressure of the cross. Jesus Christ endured it all and passed the quality control requirements. You can build your life on Him!

Unfortunately, what was meant to be the nation's greatest moment, the recognition of their Messiah, turned into their greatest sadness! The leaders apparently couldn't handle a crucified, risen Saviour. Pride, false expectations, ignorance of their own scriptures and straight out unwillingness to believe blinded them to Jesus. They stumbled over it. Two Greek words are translated 'stumble'. One has the idea of kicking against it, striking it. The other idea means being so offended it causes the person to trip and fall. Both of these words are used by Peter when writing to scattered believers. In 1 Peter 2:8 he says the stone placed in Zion, Jesus, was a 'stone that causes men to stumble and a rock that makes them fall'.

Peter does make the following quotes to excite the believers about the Stone. '... the one who trusts in him will never be put to shame.' Peter also adds, 'The stone the builders rejected has become the capstone.'

Reflection: Paul wrote, 'No one can lay any foundation other than the one already laid, which is Jesus Christ (1 Corinthians 3:11). What a privilege we have to build on Christ a life worthy of His undergirding of us.

My God is Weak
Day 20

Key verse: *We preach Christ crucified: a stumbling block to the Jews and foolishness to the Gentiles... Christ (is) the power of God and the wisdom of God...the weakness of God is stronger than man's strength' 1 Corinthians 1:23-25.*

My God is weak, so very, very weak!

He didn't break away from soldiers

Who placed the cross upon His shoulders.

My God wore their spittle and their taunts.

He must be weak to let them do such things!

My God is weak, so very, very weak!

He never fought when He was whipped.

Never threatened when He was stripped!

He stumbled, fell and the crowd laughed.

He must be weak to let them do such things!

My God is weak, so very, very weak!

No miracle to stop hammer, nail and spear

No anger to those who screamed and sneered.

Thirsty, thorn crowned, in pain He died.

He must be weak to let them do such things!

My God is weak, so very, very weak!

I'm overwhelmed by His total weakness

When He put aside His awesome greatness

To bear my shame, judgement and death!

Can He be weak to undertake such things?

My God is weak, so very, very weak!

Lifeless, entombed, salvation's hope dim

Could He in weakness overcome sin?

The empty tomb declares He 'did' win!

Can He be weak to conquer such things?

My God is weak, so very, very weak!

Yet in His weakness I find forgiveness

In His weakness I can enjoy newness.

My God's weakness is true love's greatness.

Can He be weak to achieve us such things?

My God is weak, so very, very weak!

His weakness is my celebration.

His suffering is my Salvation

His victory is my jubilation!

Can He be weak to be all those things!

My God was 'weak,'

For me and you

And I love Him for it!

Do you?

Reflection: What are some things you are humbled by when you think about God becoming weak on our behalf?

My Boast

Day 21

Key Verse: *May I never boast except in the cross of our Lord Jesus Christ, through which the world has been crucified to me, and I to the world. Galatians 6:14.*

Boasting comes naturally.

Among other things it flows from achievements, sporting or business success — or a sense of superiority. Why then would anyone want to boast about something someone else accomplished? Especially if that something offended society! Why find it praiseworthy that which exposed our moral and spiritual inadequacies before God?

We need to understand the spiritual significance in the term 'the World'. The term isn't about creation. Rather, it speaks about an atmosphere, an attitude, a realm hostile to the character and purposes of God. The apostle John warns against it. 'Do not love the world or anything in the world. If anyone loves the world, the love of the Father is not in him. For everything in the world—the cravings of sinful man, the lust of his eyes and the boasting of what he has and does—comes not from the Father but from the world' (1 John 2:15-16). These three areas sum up how Satan tempted our Lord. The plan didn't succeed. Jesus killed the disease and healed the infection of the soul at Calvary.

Those three principles still seek to infect us in different ways and with varying strength. Unfortunately, we are spiritually prone to them. Being even minutely infected and left untreated ultimately breeds hypocrisy, back-sliding and spiritual depression.

Jesus' response to the same temptations thrown at Him as to us supplies us with clues to being an Overcomer! Read Matthew 4:1-10.

Number one: 'Man does not live by bread alone, but by every word that comes from the mouth of God.' How good is my attendance at the dinner table of God?

Number two: 'Do not put the Lord your God to the test.' (The issue here is being foolish and presumptuous about God in an unethical and unbiblical manner).

Number three: 'Worship the Lord your God, and serve him only.' Here is a priority statement. It's also an insight into the set of a person's heart. Whatever we do can become an act of worship or an expression of service to our Heavenly Father.

Jesus preceded each of these statements with 'It is written…' If our Lord was sustained by the Scriptures, in this case Genesis through to Malachi, how much more we need to be strengthened from Genesis to Revelation.

We will all face the challenge of forgetting to remember. We know it causes all sorts of problems and embarrassments in life and relationships. Much of our spiritual problems also come from failing to hide God's word in our hearts through regular reading and application. The Bible constantly stresses the need for us to remember.

In this devotional we are to remember the following:

We are freed from infection's control. We still live in a diseased world which continually tries to contaminate us. Praise the Lord for the blood of Christ which continually cleanses the repentant, infected disciple.

We have a new spiritual odour. This odour is the fragrance of Christ (2 Corinthians 2:12). The world will try and smother that with its degraded smells of pleasure or prosperity.

We have a new song of hope. It's the victory song of Christ over sin, death and the devil. The world will try and silence that song through pain, persecution and poverty.

These aspects of our new life in Christ are part of our privilege in Jesus Christ. We give Him the glory even as we enjoy His gifts. The world will try and create in us spiritual dementia so as to silence our boasting about what the Lord Jesus has done in our lives.

What will protect us from forgetting to remember and thereby increase our boasting?

Growth!

This holds true at the beginning of your journey. 'Like new born babies, crave pure spiritual milk, so that you may grow up in your salvation' (1 Peter 2:2). It holds true even when you are many years down the narrow path. 'Grow in the grace and knowledge of our Lord and Saviour Jesus Christ. To him be glory both now and for ever' (2 Peter 3:18).

The summary is in Acts 2:42:'They devoted themselves to the apostle's teaching and to the fellowship, to the breaking of bread and to prayer' still applies. It is the way to remember and to grow.

Reflection: What ways are available for us to remember and to grow in our Christian life? May your life be a continual boasting about Jesus as your Lord and Saviour.

Validating the Cross

Day 22

Key verse: *Christ has indeed been raised from the dead, the first-fruits of those who have fallen asleep. 1 Corinthians 15:20.*

The word 'validate' means 'to give legal force to...' This validation is supported by the facts of the matter and confirmed by eye-witnesses. What is the validation of the work of Christ Jesus on the cross? There is really only one answer to that, the resurrection of Jesus Christ from the dead.

If there wasn't the physical resurrection of Jesus from the power of death, the tomb and the kingdom of darkness what are the consequences? Jesus is a liar! The scriptures are worthless! Salvation is a joke and the Gospel so called is a fraud!

Jesus had said 'No one takes it (His life) from me, but I lay it down of my own accord. I have authority to lay it down and authority to take it up again '(John 10:18). If there is no resurrection He has failed. In fact the verdict of the Sanhedrin that Jesus was a blasphemer would have been confirmed. The apostle Paul sums it up, 'If Christ has not been raised, our preaching is useless and so is your faith' (1 Corinthians 15:14).

We should never forget there was one simple act to destroy the fledgling followers of the Way. What was that? Simply show the people the tomb of the Nazarene. The Romans were meticulous in keeping records, so too the Jews. Revealing the body would have killed any prospective disciple's ardour as had happened to previous claimants of Messiah-ship. There was approximately forty years between the crucifixion and the destruction of Jerusalem in 70 AD. In that time no authority had exhumed the body, or charged anyone with stealing the body!

Why?

Because Jesus had risen!

Persecution by the authorities was their answer to the validation of the cross. When hardness of heart refuses to accept the truth there is only one thing left to do: destroy those whose faith, life and testimony validate

Jesus' resurrection. Why? Because transformed lives condemn those who know the facts but refuse to repent. The destruction of Jerusalem and the scattering of the nation was Satan's desperate attempt to kill off the testimony of the empty tomb.

It failed.

What then does the resurrection of Jesus validate?

The truth of Scripture and the person of Jesus!

Romans 1:2-4: 'The gospel (God) promised beforehand through his prophets in the Holy Scriptures regarding his Son, who as to his human nature was a descendant of David, and who through the Spirit of holiness was declared with power to be the Son of God, by his resurrection from the dead: Jesus Christ our Lord.'

The promises pertaining to our faith in Jesus as Saviour and Lord.

Romans 4:24-25: '… God will credit righteousness – for us who believe in him who raised Jesus our Lord from the dead. He was delivered over to death for our sins and was raised to life for our justification.' The resurrection is an essential factor in our believing and confessing Jesus Christ as Lord and Saviour. We declare Jesus isn't a ghost! He rose from the dead with a glorified, tangible body, visible, recognisable, embraceable!

The hope of a new destiny as well as His presence with us through this life.

1 Peter 1:3-5: 'Praise be to the God and Father of our Lord Jesus Christ! In his great mercy he has given us new birth into a living hope through the resurrection of Jesus Christ from the dead, and into an inheritance that can never perish, spoil or fade – kept in heaven for you, who through faith are shielded by God's power until the coming of the salvation that is ready to be revealed in the last time.'

It gives to the Church's two sacraments meaning and assurance of His victory.

1 Peter 3:21-22: 'This water (the deluge of the flood) symbolises baptism that now saves you also – not the removal of dirt from the body but the pledge of a good conscience towards God. It saves you by the resurrection of Jesus who has gone into heaven and is at God's right hand…'

1 Corinthians 10:16: 'Is not the cup of thanksgiving for which we give thanks a participation in the blood of Christ? And is not the bread that we break a participation in the body of Christ?' Paul then goes on to say in chapter 11:26: 'For whenever you eat this bread and drink this cup, you proclaim the Lord's death until he comes.' For Him to fulfil the promise of coming again to establish the Kingdom of God on earth, He must have risen from the tomb.

Reflection: Do I appreciate the privilege of validating the person and work of Christ? Do I celebrate the wonder that because He lives, I have eternal life, *now?*

Racism and the Cross
Day 23

Key Verse: *All of you who were baptised into Christ have clothed yourselves with Christ. There is neither Jew nor Greek, slave nor free, male nor female, for you are all one in Christ Jesus. Galatians 3:26-27.*

Racism is the monster created by ethnic pride and fed by evolutionary theory. Trying to defend racial differences, colours and culture can breed superiority and inferiority illusions. The biblical account of creation and salvation destroys any such impression. The message of the cross to humankind actually lays down the foundation for racial and gender equality. As a Pharisee, Saul (later he used his Roman name, Paul) considered himself superior not only to the debased Gentiles, but also to the commoner of Jewish descent. What a dramatic change took place when his life was turned upside down, inside out, cleansed, renewed by the risen Jesus Christ.

The letter to the Ephesians holds within itself the unequalled doctrine of God's grace. Here is written the very power of the cross in dealing with the delusion of racial superiority and religious elitism. Paul tackles head-on the debasement of morality and spirituality in the Gentile world (Ephesians 2:1-3). He also attacks the self-righteous conceit of Israel's obsession with its commandments and regulations (Ephesians 2:15).

How could the Lord Jesus bridge this divide? How could He deal with the sin inherent in one, and the sin which permeated the other? How could Jesus bring two opposing minds, Gentile and Jewish, together? Only by taking both to and through a death experience and bringing them into a new united life and relationship! How could this be possible? Only by the power of the cross and resurrection of Jesus, and by placing both under a new Headship!

The Bible is insistent that God created one man named Adam. Through him and his wife Eve came all humanity. Through him also came sin and death, condemnation and judgement because he was our Federal Head. 'Sin entered the world through one man, and death through sin, and in this way death came to all men, because all have sinned...' (Romans 5:12). To overcome this problem caused by Adam, one man, Jesus, took on those issues and paid the cost at Calvary, 'If the many died by the trespass of the one man, how much more did God's grace and the gift that came by the grace of the one man, Jesus Christ, overflow to the many' (Romans 5:15)!

Abraham was chosen, according to Genesis 12:3, so all peoples on earth would be blessed. All means *all*. Throughout both Testaments are stories of individuals outside the appointed nation with whom God had dealings, such as Job, Melchizedek, Cyrus and Nebuchadnezzar. In the Gospels we are treated to the mystery of the Magi, the Samaritan woman at the well in John 4, the Syro-Phoenician woman with a demon possessed daughter (Mark 7:24-30). The Greeks who sought Him out and the accounts of the Roman centurions all testify to Christ's acceptance.

The barrier between the Jewish mindset and the Gentile world is best revealed in the Lord's dealing with Peter. Acts 10 is devoted to this wrestle to overcome the prejudice which lurks within. Peter was hungry and fell into a trance. The Lord impressed upon Peter's mind a huge sheet filled with animals not eaten by Jews. Peter refused, using his excuse about ritual purity. God told him not to call things unclean which God had purified. Peter was confused as he wondered what it meant. Then the knock on the door! Gentile servants of Cornelius came to invite Peter to share the Gospel with this Roman centurion. Lesson learnt, accepted, applied! Peter went and a whole family and household accepted Christ as Lord and Saviour. This lesson had to be learnt by others and it wasn't easy or accepted without a battle and a price paid. The battle still rages and, unfortunately, some pay a high price when they accept God's teaching!

Ephesians 2:13-18 is the best reply. 'Now in Christ Jesus you who once were far away have been brought near through the blood of Christ. For he himself is our peace, who has made the two (Jew and Gentile) one and has destroyed the barrier, the dividing wall of hostility, by abolishing in his flesh the law with its commandments and regulations. His purpose was to create in himself one new man out of the two, thus making peace, and in one body to reconcile both of them to God through the cross, by which he put to death their hostility...For through him we both have access to the Father by one Spirit.'

Reflection: Think about those from another country and culture who have been a blessing to you in word and deed. Give thanks to God right now for the oneness of the Christian family.

Good News

Day 24

Key verse: '*I am not ashamed of the gospel, because it is the power of God for the salvation of everyone who believes: first for the Jew, then for the Gentile.' Romans* 1:16.

How could it be good news?

The man was indicted as a blasphemer by leaders of his own nation. He was labelled as a seditious person by the occupying Roman power. He was betrayed by one of His own, rejected by His countrymen who were more interested in blood-sport than truth and justice.

Jesus received more than simply bad press. He encountered unjust verdicts and condemnation from leaders intent upon self preservation. Despised, rejected, unpitied, he was crucified and written off as another failed would-be Messiah.

How could this be good news?

When writing to the Corinthian disciples Paul unveiled the foundation by which the events surrounding Jesus are determined as good news. 'What I received I passed on to you as of first importance; that Christ died for our sins according to the Scriptures, that He was buried, that He was raised on the third day according to the Scriptures' (1Corinthians 15:3-4). Within these verses are some precious 'paving stones' essential for an unshakeable foundation.

Applying the title Christ to Jesus emphasises His being anointed to the role of Redeemer. 'The Spirit of the Lord is on me, because he has anointed me to preach good news to the poor. He has sent me to proclaim freedom to the prisoners and recovery of sight for the blind, to release the oppressed, to proclaim the year of the Lord's favour' (Luke 4:18-19 quoting Isaiah 61:1-2).

This Christ died!

Nothing unusual about that at first glance, except He chose to die on behalf of others! It was in a public manner with no room for accusations of easy, painless execution. Whether a person believes it or not the verdict concerning the reason for Christ's death was to pay the penalty of sin, that is, death (Romans 6:23a). Jesus' action was no spur of the moment matter. He knew the scriptures. He knew His mission. From Genesis through to Malachi the thread of a suffering, dying Messiah can be seen. Psalm 22 and Isaiah 53 are two prominent examples. The sheer number of prophecies, typologies, parables and statements to this event destroys any attempt of a conspiracy by Jesus' disciples after the crucifixion.

According to the scriptures the Christ was not only going to be put to death but also buried to rise again. On the day of ingathering, the Pentecost festival, the apostle Peter declared this glorious truth. He asserted not his opinion but the words of the Hebrew scriptures. Psalm 16:8-11 and Psalm 110:1 were quoted by Peter who explained their words could not refer to David whose tomb they knew. The Psalms spoke about not seeing decay and of sitting at the right hand of the Lord God. These words could only refer to the one they knew as Jesus. He who was crucified had been ordained as Messiah by His rising from the tomb. This was foretold by Jesus who spoke about the sign of Jonah in Matthew 12:39-41, 16:4.

The foundation for the good news had been laid in the Hebrew scriptures over hundreds of years. Any fair-minded person could easily understand the impossibility of any human fingerprint in this drama of salvation. The eternal God alone could plan, oversee and complete such a wonderful redemption in the face of Satan's opposition and humanity's unbelief and fickleness.

So then, on such a foundation how do we perceive the good news personally? Surely it means God is true to His Word. Jesus died on the Cross to deliver all who trust in Him from the wrath of God, eternal separation from His presence and the guilt, shame and power of sin in their earthly living. 'Therefore, there is now no condemnation for those who are in Christ Jesus, because through Christ Jesus the law of the Spirit of life set me free from the law of sin and death. For what the Law was powerless to do in that it was weakened by the sinful nature, God did by sending his own Son in the likeness of sinful man to be a sin offering' Romans 8:1-3.

Now that is Good News!

Reflection: What other aspects of the death, burial and resurrection of Christ Jesus makes the message of the Cross good news to me?

The Suffering and the Glory.
Day 25

Key verse: *Praise be to the God and Father of our Lord Jesus Christ! In his great mercy he has given us new birth into a living hope through the resurrection of Jesus Christ from the dead. 1 Peter 1:3.*

A good mystery has many clues pointing to the person or persons under investigation. The same applies to the Old Testament. Within its pages a mystery man was indicated as the promised Messiah. Hundreds of years rolled by and still the prophets and people of God continued to try and uncover who he was. They were 'trying to find out the time and circumstances...predicted (of) the sufferings of Christ and the glories that would follow' (1 Peter 1:11).

Notice the order: suffering, then glory. The students of the Old Testament knew about Psalm 22 and Isaiah 53 with their pictures of suffering and substitution. The Messiah's glory was highlighted in such passages as Psalm 2 and Nebuchadnezzar's dream in Daniel 2.

What previous generations wanted to know, Peter declared could now be known. All the clues pointed to Jesus. By implication, Peter is saying: look at the clues. Weigh them up in the light of historical events and you will solve the mystery. The clues find fulfilment in Jesus. He is the suffering servant of Isaiah 53. He is the anguished person who cried, 'My God, my God, why have your forsaken me' in Psalm 22.

The fisherman of Galilee once rebuked Jesus for speaking about the cross (Matthew 16:21-23). Now Peter fills his letter with the message of the cross. The reclamation of Peter from bitter failure is one of the most touching events associated with the resurrection. By the sea of Galilee Peter's three denials of his Lord is redressed by Jesus recommissioning him three times (John 21).

What was the cost of being reclaimed from the empty way of life handed down from generation to generation? Not with material wealth! Redemption could only come through the poured out life of the spotless Lamb. Peter had been introduced to Him by John the Baptist (John 1) and had scrutinised

Him for three years. Peter wasn't naïve, he knew the scriptures. For him, Jesus was the promised One, the Messiah.

What did the apostle mean when he wrote about being redeemed from an empty, vain, fruitless life? Simply put, a life without Jesus is a life of slavery to passions which degrade; of ignorance which blocks out Truth; an emptiness of meaning which dehumanises self and others. You could write those points over so much of our society. The era has changed, not the soul nature.

It is into this type of world the gospel burst with its alternative offer to searchers after truth, holiness and hope. It was of a Redeemer whose long promised suffering was now fulfilled. Now His glory was assured. In a world without hope we have a living hope. We see beyond the brutality and corruption of the 'now' to an inheritance secured for us by the very death of our Saviour. It is an inheritance which can never perish, spoil or fade. Peter lets us know there's a reservation sign on it with our names attached. Peter must have had in mind John 14:2-3: 'In my Father's house are many rooms…I am going there to prepare a place for you. And if I go and prepare a place for you, I will come back and take you to be with me that you also may be where I am.'

As you read what they wrote remember it is still valid. What was to be theirs is to be ours on the same ground—the shed blood of Christ and His resurrection Whenever you are under pressure to back-track on your commitment to Christ take your mind to Calvary. Remember Christ Jesus suffered there for you. There He endured insults and more, much more. There He bore our sins and all the consequences of such a burden. There He prayed for you and me. There He opened the gate to glory for any who would receive Him as Lord and Saviour.

Remember that day!

It puts whatever you or I experience into perspective: time against eternity, loss in the light of gain, emptiness overcome by meaning.

Reflection: When you claimed Jesus as your Messiah and Lord you solved the mystery of the Old Testament. There are still many things to discover about Jesus from His Word. May you enjoy searching out these things!

The Cross and the Coming King
Day 26

Key verses: *The grace of God that brings salvation has appeared to all men. It teaches us to say 'No' to ungodliness and worldly passions, and to live self-controlled, upright and godly lives in this present age, while we wait for the blessed hope—the glorious appearing of our great God and Saviour, Jesus Christ. Titus 2:11-13.*

At the Passover celebration there were four cups of wine drunk throughout the meal. Jesus mentioned two of the four cups. One He said represented the blood of the new covenant. The other, the cup of acceptance, would be drunk again in the kingdom of God (Matthew 26:27-29).

Between the cups stood the cross and the age of grace. Why couldn't the kingdom arrive without the cross? Why were the hosts of heaven prevented from invading the kingdom of darkness and setting up the throne in Zion? Because the dominion of death, sin's judgement and humanity's transformation and forgiveness had not been dealt with! Only the cross could solve those issues.

Pilate put a sign over the crucified, thorn-crowned head of Jesus. 'This is Jesus, the King of the Jews' (Matthew 27:37). Historically and biblically true, what Pilate wrote was also a prophetic statement. He didn't realise, however, the full truth of that which he wrote. For Jesus is the king of the Jews, indeed, of the whole house of Israel. One day it will extend to a universal reign. 'The Lord will be king over the whole earth. On that day there will be one Lord and his name the only name' (Zechariah 14:9). The crown of thorns will give way to many crowns and He will be called, 'King of Kings and Lord of Lords' (Revelation 19:16).

How will the world know the rightful Ruler when He comes? Zechariah provided some clues long before the cross, 'The house of David and the inhabitants of Jerusalem …will look on me, the one they have pierced…' (Zechariah 12:10). What are those wounds? In John 20:24-29 is the account of Thomas the apostle, who came to understand what it meant. From his experience we, too, understand! It was when the risen Lord appeared and showed His hands and side to the doubter the mystery was solved. The wounds of the cross are the insignia of the King of Kings and Lord of Lords. They cannot be duplicated! In Revelation 5 Jesus is the central figure in the throne room of Glory. He is described as the Lamb with the appearance of one slain. This could only refer to the wounds of His pierced hands, feet and side.

When the Lord ascended to heaven He promised to return the same way and to the same place of departure (Acts 1:11). In Zechariah 14:4 you will notice the link: 'On that day (the Lord's) feet will stand on the Mount of Olives east of Jerusalem...' The claim is unmistakeable, Jesus is the Lord!

Scripture tells us that 'Today is the day of Salvation'. It is a period of time whose limit is known only to God. The 'next day', therefore, will be the day of judgement. Its length is not stated, but will be much shorter than the day of grace. The Word of God has more to say about the return of the King than it does about His coming as the suffering Servant. The promised 'next day' will not be a pleasant time for some. Revelation 1:7: 'Look, he is coming with the clouds, and every eye will see him, even those who pierced him; and all the peoples of the earth will mourn because of him. So shall it be! Amen.' However, 'On the day he comes to be glorified in his holy people and to be marvelled at among all those who have believed. This includes you, because you believed our testimony to you' (2 Thessalonians 1:10). The difference between the two verses is positive faith in or negative faith about Jesus Christ.

Without the Lord's crucifixion there could only be wrath poured out upon creation! Because of the triumph of the Messiah we look forward to the atmosphere of heaven taking over the realm of earth. Then will come true what we quote around Christmas time. 'Of the increase of his government and peace there will be no end. He will reign on David's throne and over his kingdom, establishing and upholding it with justice and righteousness from that time on and for ever. The zeal of the Lord Almighty will accomplish this' (Isaiah 9:7).

Reflection: Have I given any serious attention to what the Bible says about the return of the crucified Lord? Why does Paul call this our 'blessed hope' (Titus 2:13)?

The Foolishness of God

Day 27

Verses: *We preach Christ Crucified: a stumbling–block to Jews and foolishness to Gentiles, but to whom God has called, both Jews and Greeks, Christ the power of God and the wisdom of God. For the foolishness of God is wiser than man's wisdom, and the weakness of God is stronger than man's strength. 1 Corinthians 1:23-25.*

Corinth hadn't heard anything like this before. It was enough to catch their attention, ponder and then make them laugh out loud. This cosmopolitan city, with its philosophers and debauched religions, must have considered a message of the cross stupid. Belief in a crucified Messiah was surely doomed to oblivion, and soon!

The idea of God becoming man wasn't unique. Greek mythology had already corrupted the scriptural promise through its legends and fables. The problem was in God going to all the trouble to send His Son as a substitute sacrifice for humanity. The apostle spoke about God's love and this was a concept foreign to their belief system. Their idea of gods precluded any concept of unconditional love. Lust, yes! Power, yes! Sport, yes! Love, no, no, no! They would find it impossible to equate the gods of mount Olympus with the God of Calvary. What John wrote in his first letter is inconceivable. 'This is love: not that we loved God, but that he loved us and sent his Son as an atoning sacrifice for our sins' (1 John 4:10). A nice idea, but unrealistic to the Greeks!

Such foolishness, however, could not be laughed away. It challenged the philosophical wisdom of the age. Why did the crucified Christ make God look foolish in the thinking of the people, especially the cultured and esteemed philosophers?

The body beautiful was all the rage in Greece. Athletic contests featured strong, robust, energetic men competing for the winner's garland. Beautiful statues graced the city whilst their religion honoured gods of war, intrigue and power. The Greeks also were enamoured by theories, debates and various religious concepts. Paul's assessment of such wisdom as hollow and deceptive was because they depended upon human tradition and worldly principles (Colossians 2:8). The result? A slave to vanity!

Into this scene comes the message of the Messiah who was led as a lamb to the slaughter. He was battered beyond recognition and never retaliated. This Jesus never even cursed. He didn't swear revenge on those who betrayed Him, tortured Him and crucified Him. Rather, His cry was 'Forgive them.' How foolish can God be? Why would He be willing to appear a clown rather than a vengeful martyr?

Jesus Christ crucified violates the arrogance of men and women. They imagine it is possible to impress God with their knowledge, wisdom and achievements. The gospel declared the need of a perfect substitute who is named Jesus. This arouses the ire of the ego and the wrath of self-righteousness. Worse still, declare Jesus is God's Son and it seems more ridiculous.

Where then is the wisdom of God woven in the Gospel? To know God's thoughts requires the Spirit of God. Without Him the crucified Jesus remains a foolish proclamation. Therefore in the wisdom of God the foolish message becomes the assessor of the soul. There is no better testimony to the wisdom and power of God than His becoming weak in His Son Jesus to bear the sin of the world. There is no greater wisdom than God destroying the philosophical vanity of a self-righteous and corrupt world through the proclamation of the cross. How? Because from beginning to end salvation is the work of God! The only boasting allowed in God's presence is in what Jesus has done historically and personally.

The power and effectiveness of this foolish message is recorded in 1 Corinthians 6:9-11: 'Do you not know that the wicked will not inherit the kingdom of God? Do not be deceived: Neither the sexually immoral nor idolaters nor adulterers nor male prostitutes nor homosexual offenders nor thieves nor the greedy nor drunkards nor slanderers nor swindlers will inherit the kingdom of God. And that is what some of you were. But you were washed, you were sanctified, you were justified in the name of the Lord Jesus Christ and by the Spirit of our God.'

Reflection: What is the best testimony that what the world calls foolishness is actually God's wisdom and power?

Those Symbolised around the Cross
Day 28

Key verse: *Many bulls surround me; strong bulls of Bashan encircle me. Roaring lions tearing their prey open their mouths wide against me. Psalm 22:12-13.*

The psalmist's graphic imagery confronts and arouses strong emotions. From Psalm 22 we gain a poetic and symbolic picture of some of the protagonists around the cross. The four Gospels each have their own unique emphasis and must be read together to drink in the scene. When you compare the Psalm with Jesus' historical experience you gain a deeper insight into His confrontation with evil.

The man from Galilee is symbolised in this Psalm as a worm (the term for 'worm' is used for the crimson coccus worm from which the scarlet dye was obtained). The savage intent of the evil forces lined up against Him are symbolised as wild bulls, well pastured bulls of Bashan, dogs and lions. The scene is weighted in evil's favour. The worm's hope of escape was less than zero.

The Bulls of Bashan are the sleek and well fed creatures who, both from curiosity and fear, gape, roar and want to impale the one before them. Could these be compared with the chief priests and rulers who mocked Him and challenged Him to descend from the cross? In their view this teacher and healer was an upstart who threatened, not only their position and religious status, but also the nation. It was stated at their meeting, 'What are we accomplishing? Here is this man performing many miraculous signs. If we let him go on like this, everyone will believe in him, and then the Romans will come and take away both our place and our nation. Then one of them, named Caiaphas, who was high priest that year, spoke up "you know nothing at all! You do not realise that it is better for you that one man die for the people than that the whole nation perish." ' (John11:47-50).

The dogs which surround are the unclean scavengers of ancient society. Surely, these depict the Roman soldiers who carried out the piercing of hands and feet. They also dispersed the few garments He possessed. The soldiers mocked Him. They did, however, offer Him drugged wine to ease the terrible pain. This Jesus refused!

One of the most awesome aspects of the crucifixion is the fact of Jesus 'the Worm' praying for those 'creatures' and others intent on destroying Him. He never laid a charge of wilfulness against them. His prayer availed, at least for some such as the Roman who exclaimed, 'Surely this was a righteous man'. It also liberated the thief who asked to be remembered when Jesus came to claim His kingdom. The Lord replied that the thief would be with Him that very day in paradise. Joseph, who was on the council, and Nicodemus also benefited from Christ's prayer! In fact, you and I were also included in the most awesome, powerful and gracious prayer ever offered.

The roaring lions must surely point to the unseen, but very evident, presence of the devil. In Peter's letter the devil is called the roaring lion who seeks to devour. Here was Satan's one and only opportunity to win the war. The battle of the Lion and the Worm was underway. To all observers it seemed a foregone conclusion, especially as the days in the tomb ticked over. There wasn't any way known that Jesus 'the worm' would prevail over the devil as the roaring lion. By the power of the Father's promise, and the sinlessness of Jesus, 'the Worm' thrashed the lion. Defeated, he has not yet been caged in the bottomless pit (Revelation 20).

The Worm was scorned and despised. He was mocked and insulted. He was the weakest of all. He triumphed over all. How was this possible? The Lord Jesus trusted in the faithfulness of God the Father. His fulfilling of the law would mean death had no power to lock Him in the tomb. He paid the penalty for our sin and judgement, yet His righteous life was not conquered by them. He did cry out to the Father and in the agony of judgement felt alone. But His cry was heard!

The Worm won!

On the cross Jesus was the weakest creature in the universe. His weakness is greater than all the might of all the peoples of all time. Now He is more than the weakest of creatures. He is the Lord of Lords, the Almighty before whom we all will bow.

Reflection: Job 25:6 asks how a person can be pure in God's sight, for humanity is but a worm? Psalm 22 and its fulfilment answers that question. The eternal Son of God became a worm for us so that we might become the person God intended.

The Personal Mystery of the Cross

Day 29

Key verse: *Now if we died with Christ, we believe that we will also live with him. Romans 6:8.*

According to the Gospels two others were crucified with Christ. From a doctrinal viewpoint there were many more. In fact, to be a member of His Body, the Church, you must have experienced the personal mystery of the cross. This is hard to grasp. The mind finds it hard to comprehend while the heart embraces it by faith.

Without the personal reality of being co-crucified with Christ there is absolutely no possibility of belonging to Him. The New Testament gives us the assurance that, from our identification with Christ's death and burial, we will also rise to be with Him.

Christ's victory at Calvary didn't eliminate Satan, sin, the curse and condemnation of the Mosaic Law. What Jesus as the Son of Man accomplished was our death to them! Jesus collected sin's wages: death! Jesus satisfied the Father's wrath! Jesus silenced Satan's accusations! Jesus, our Lord and Saviour, was now able to take us with Him into a new realm. This dimension is the Kingdom of Light (Colossians 1:13). When we embraced Jesus we began a walk with Him. This journey is in the Light of Life over which the kingdom of darkness has no control (John 8:12).

How was this brought about? By the Gospel, once foretold, now fulfilled in Christ Jesus and proclaimed by His servants! What is the prerequisite for exchanging the realm of darkness for the light of life? Romans 10:8-10 is a summary: 'The word is near you; it is in your mouth and in your heart, that is, the word of faith we are proclaiming. That if you confess with your mouth 'Jesus is Lord', and believe in your heart that God raised him from the dead, you will be saved. For it is with your heart that you believe and are justified, and it is with your mouth that you confess and are saved.'

Coming to that conviction has different effects upon different people. In many ways we undergo our own struggles, if not in a garden of Gethsemane, then in a barren wilderness or turbulent mountainside. The devil throws all his resources at us. He digs up our past and present unworthiness and reminds us of all we stand to lose in fame, fortune and pleasure. Only the power of Christ's love, forgiveness and promise to share our new life breaks the spell of the darkness. When we cry out to the Lord, the Holy Spirit moves our inner being and destiny into the Body of Christ (1 Corinthians 12:13)!

Now we are able to say with the apostle Paul, 'I have been crucified with Christ and I no longer live, but Christ lives in me. The life I live in the body, I live by faith in the Son of God, who loved me and gave himself for me' (Galatians 2:20).

All this takes place in the unseen dimensions of the spirit. The kingdom of God and the kingdom of Satan are the only witnesses to what took place in your life and mine. Has the Lord God given to us something tangible within our physical world to express our change of kingdoms? Without it we may well be infected with crippling doubts, especially when the world, the flesh and the Devil assault us.

What then is our defence? Christ Jesus! When we stumble who lifts us up? Christ Jesus! When we prevail what is our boast? Christ Jesus! What is our anthem? 'Thanks be to God! He gives us the victory through our Lord Jesus Christ' (1 Corinthians 15:57).

In Romans 6 and elsewhere we are given the most wonderful, the most dramatic and the most satisfying physical expression of our spiritual experience! It's the Christian act of baptism by immersion in water. This demonstrates vividly what the Holy Spirit has done for us. He has placed us in Christ. We share His death and burial. Being brought up and out of the water is a symbol of coming with Christ out of the tomb. Now we can live out that victory by the way we learn to walk as children of the Light.

As we journey our lifestyle will undergo changes. The personal mystery of our union with Jesus Christ at the cross spreads it influence over every aspect of our lives.

Reflection: As a disciple in the kingdom of Light am I discovering the mystery of my personal identification with Jesus on the cross?

Heaven's Song of Calvary
Day 30

Key verse: *I heard every creature in heaven and on earth and under the earth and on the sea, and all that is in them, singing: To him who sits on the throne and to the Lamb be praise and honour and glory and power for ever and ever! Revelation 5:1-13.*

We are told there is music throughout the universe. Astronomers can hear the music from the stars, each one with its own tune. On the day when Jesus died on Golgotha's hill I wonder if the music ceased.

For three days only the discordant sounds of darkness would have reverberated through outer space as the body of the Christ lay entombed. What a change would have taken place to those with ears to hear on the morning when Jesus rose from the dead. I imagine the angels of heaven singing and dancing for joy as they beheld the Lord of Glory. What a reception awaited Jesus when He ascended to the right hand side of the Father.

In Revelation the apostle John is given a front seat reservation for the heavenly choir's presentation. It was a musical celebration of the Lamb. We read the account as events yet to unfold and rightly so. The angels, elders and others proclaim it as a story ready to be fulfilled! How thrilling is this preview of a musical extravaganza of praise which will be ours to join at God's chosen time.

What was their song all about? 'I saw a Lamb, looking as if it had been slain, standing in the centre of the throne, encircled by the four living creatures…' (Revelation 5:6). Here was the Lamb of God who takes away the sin of the world. How would he do that? Through His sacrifice and resurrection victory! That song from the massed choir of heaven was one which could never have been sung before Calvary.

'You are worthy…' is the opening refrain. Why was He worthy of such acclaim? He left His glory for the realm of humanity and humbled Himself as a slave. He stood the tests of life and death yet did not sin. He carried the condemnation of God the Father's judgement on our sin and was

not consumed. He rose again and robbed hades and death of their power (Revelation 1:18).

'Because you were slain...' is the theme. Why was He slain? Not as a martyr, but as a substitute. Not without significance, but in fulfilment of prophecy and symbolism. It was not due to the injustice of human authority but according to the divine plan.

'With your blood you purchased men (and women) for God...' declares the purpose. Some, with tender sensitivities, recoil from the term 'blood'. It is, however, very graphic in its imagery, yet it simply means the poured out life of the person (Leviticus 7:14). On the cross, Jesus, Son of Man, became the price of our redemption from sin, death and condemnation. The song goes on to say:

'From every tribe and language and people and nation...' This means He has included you! There is no corner of earth not covered by the grace, love and sacrifice of Jesus Christ. From every part there will be those who will rejoice in being redeemed by the poured out life of Christ at Calvary.

'You have made them to be a kingdom and priests to serve our God...' proclaims the result. We are not only saved from sin's control and thereby eternal rejection from God's presence. We are raised up as a kingdom of priests. This allows us to worship and serve our Lord and Saviour in His presence, face to face, forever. Hallelujah!

The Lord who triumphed at Calvary turned earth's tragedy into heaven's anthem of praise. What the angels sang about as witnesses we can sing about as recipients. For we have become the ones He has purchased. We are His. We are precious to Him. He redeemed us at a price beyond our comprehension. We can join in and sing the angels' song. We can declare that Jesus has turned our death into life, our tragedy into triumph, our despair into delight.

We should all look forward to the day Revelation 5:13 records: 'Then I heard every creature in heaven and on earth and under the earth and on the sea, and all that is in them, singing, To him who sits on the throne and to the Lamb be praise and honour and glory and power, for ever and ever!'

Reflection: Can you write your own song of praise to Jesus? If not, which of the songs that you know do you like best?

My Personal Cross
Day 31

Key verse: *Then he said to them all: 'If anyone would come after me, he must deny himself and take up his cross daily and follow me'. Luke 9:23.*

Shocked would have been an understatement. Two unexpected verbal 'punches' landed on the chins of the disciples. One was Christ's announcement that he was to be betrayed and crucified. That was shocking enough. Then He follows through with the cost of being His disciple.

The cross was loathed, feared, and an object of shame. Being the Roman authority's chosen method of capital punishment, the hearers must have quaked in their sandals. What was Jesus asking of them? What is He continuing to ask of us? Within the Gospels are two specific mentions of Jesus confronting people with this challenge. To read the accounts may help us interpret Christ's meaning.

When talking to the twelve Jesus linked the cross to a choice: gaining the world, being ashamed of Jesus to preserve one's own life, or putting all that to death to follow Him! Later, the Lord expanded on this choice. Before His own crucifixion Jesus talked to those with Him after the Passover meal. 'All this I have told you so that you will not go astray. They will put you out of the synagogue; in fact, a time is coming when anyone who kills you will think he is offering a service to God' (John 16:1-2).

On another occasion a large crowd followed Jesus. He easily attracted a crowd. Curious onlookers gathered around Him. They did not impress Him with their superficial support. He sifted them by a confrontation with the cross. Discipleship has serious implications on family relationships. It's important to realise the close knit culture of eastern family relationships and what Jesus required. To be His disciple meant possibly foregoing the family unit. As such, that would be considered as a hatred of kith and kin. Jesus claimed total allegiance. Then the Master went on to say, 'Anyone who does not carry his cross and follow me cannot be my disciple' (Luke 14:27).

What do you think is the cross in such a situation?

Is it still being played out today?

Confronted by the invitation of Jesus to follow Him under *His* conditions becomes a trust issue. How well do we know the One who calls us to the denial of our independence? How sure are we about taking up the symbol of shame and death?

Handing over our self-government to the Lord's government isn't easy. Jesus doesn't ask for a Lenten experience for forty days. He asks us to trust Him for everything and in everything.

In the days before the welfare society people understood dependence. Today, in our western world, we can relax in the welfare state. 'Lord, give us this day our daily bread' is almost a foreign concept even to those who sincerely pray the Lord's Prayer. When Jesus challenges us with our own cross it challenges our personal sovereignty! Do I have confidence in Jesus as my Lord, to guide me through life with its tough or placid times, and bless me as He sees fit?

Christ Jesus doesn't throw crosses at us as if they were confetti. Each one is personalised! When He points out the one for us it has been crafted in its rugged way to suit our personality, calling and faith. Each of us will have to handle varying degrees of shame and loss. There will be all manner of death experiences, from ambition, inheritance and for some, life itself. Is following Jesus worth it?

When He is our Master He walks us up the narrow way, beginning at our own Calvary. Do we believe Him to be the Christ, the Son of God, our Saviour and Lord? Do we believe He has our best interest at heart?To say 'YES!' is to find the surrender of self and the acceptance of our individual crosses much easier to handle. Why? Calvary!

The words of the apostle Paul sums up our attitude to our personal cross, 'I consider everything loss compared to the surpassing greatness of knowing Christ Jesus my Lord, for whose sake I have lost all things. I consider them rubbish that I may gain Christ…' (Philippians 3:8).

Reflection: Are there things or issues in my life which makes carrying my personalised cross hard going? What must I do to regain the joy which makes the weight of the cross insignificant?

Heaven's Song to the Lamb

Revelation 4 and 5

The throne room of glory
Rang out the wonderful story
As the angels sang of Calvary
And the Lamb that was slain!

Glory and praise to the Lamb!
Glory and power to His Name!
He, Lamb of God, was slain
Men and women to reclaim
Glory and majesty to the Lamb!

The hallways of Heaven
With their victory song did ring
As thousands and thousands could sing
To the Lamb that was slain.

Glory and honour belong to Him
Glory and power to His Name
He, the Lamb of God, was slain
Men and women now proclaim.
Glory and honour unto the Lamb!

The mansions of glory
Hear the redeemed rejoicing
Their salvation songs exalting
The Lamb who for them was slain!

Glory and honour belong to Him!
Glory and power to his Name!
Jesus the Lamb of God slain
Men and women reclaimed
Glory and worship give to the Lamb

Discussion Topics

After concluding the 31 Day Devotional on Captured by Calvary you might like to pursue some of the subject matter a little further. This could be done as a solo exercise or by forming a small group to share your insights.

The following are starters. You or others may like to walk down some other tracks which have opened up as areas for spiritual investigation on the theme of the cross.

Discussion starter 1

Why was the Cross necessary?

Do you think God had other options?

Why?

Consider devotional days 1, 13, 21.

Discussion starter 2

In what ways has the cross revealed the impotency of Satan and his kingdom?

Consider devotional days 3, 14, 15, 21.

Discussion starter 3

Jesus is called 'The Lamb of God'. What does it mean?

Is there some aspect of this title which is precious to you?

Consider devotional days 2, 6, 7, 30.

Discussion starter 4

To follow Jesus requires us to 'take up our cross'. What does this mean?

What is associated with taking up our cross?

Are all our crosses the same?

Why?

Consider devotional days 17, 23, 26, 31.

www.ingramcontent.com/pod-product-compliance
Lightning Source LLC
Chambersburg PA
CBHW071029080526
44587CB00015B/2544

Advent was at one time a dour season of prayer, fasting and penitence. For me a distinct melancholy hangs over our grey rainy islands during December's darkening days. Some people just enjoy the telly and the partying, and others doubtless try to ignore the whole thing. But I think there are also those who, like me, spend the festive season running an emotional gamut. Underlying the commercial clamour there's a nostalgic sense of loss; a wistfulness - not for how it used to be in Christmases past, but for how it might have been and never really was.

Adventus: the coming. These twenty-five poems reflect on Christmases past and current, on lives lived, on endings of years and of relationships; on beginnings, anxieties, hopes, and an uncertain future.

Though these poems are perennials, they also serve as daily readings starting from the first day of December.

Sue Vickerman

Also by Sue Vickerman

Poetry

Shag
Arrowhead Press 2003; Naked Eye Publishing, 2017

The social decline of the oystercatcher,
Biscuit Publishing, England, 2005

Kunst by 'Suki', Indigo Dreams Publishing, England, 2012

Thin bones like wishbones by 'Suki' and Sue Vickerman,
Indigo Dreams Publishing, England, 2013

Fiction

Special needs, Cinnamon Press, Wales, 2011

A small life, Cinnamon Press, Wales, 2012

Two small lives, Naked Eye Publishing, England, 2016

True Life Nude, to be published by Naked Eye, 2018

Online fiction
asmalllife.co.uk
twosmalllives.co.uk
truelifenude.co.uk

Blog
sukithelifemodel.co.uk